Praise for *Before the World Intruded*

"Michele is a courageous heroine, but she's also very accessible.
She explores the darkest days of her life with a brave, open heart,
tirelessly learning painful lessons, which she shares with
an engaging vulnerability. When she finally dances into a life
free of trauma, we dance alongside Michele happily.
I loved her generosity and humanity
in this important, beautiful book."

—Priscilla Warner, author of *Learning to Breathe:
My Yearlong Quest to Bring Calm to My Life*
and co-author of the bestselling *The Faith Club*

"Whenever I feel sad that I've finished a book,
I know I've been transformed by its pages.
Michele's story is incredibly moving, and beautifully written.
. . . her prose is rich, descriptive and fluid off the tongue."

—Deborah Serani, PsyD, author of *Living with Depression:
Why Biology and Biography Matter on the Path to Hope and Healing*

"A sad but ultimately uplifting story, told simply and powerfully,
that all of us should listen to and learn from."

—David Biro, MD, PhD, author of *100 Days: My Unexpected Journey
from Doctor to Patient*

"...there are lessons to be learned from Michele
that will benefit everyone."

—Alex Pattakos, PhD, author of *Prisoners of Our Thoughts*
(from the foreword)

"*Before the World Intruded* is a gift. One woman's journey of
healing gives all of us the hope and inspiration to make changes
in our own lives. Mic͟h͟ ͟ ͟ ͟ ͟ ͟v͟e͟s that no challenge is too difficult
to overcome—e ͟ ͟ ͟ ͟ ͟ ͟ ͟ ͟ ͟ ͟ ͟ ͟ ͟ ͟ ͟ ͟ ͟ ͟ ͟ind.
This book will mov͟ ͟ ͟ ͟ ͟ ͟ ͟ ͟ ͟ ͟ ͟ ͟ ͟ ͟ ͟ ͟ourse of
his or her life, an͟ ͟ ͟ ͟ ͟ ͟ ͟ ͟ ͟ ͟ ͟ ͟ ͟ ͟ ͟cess."

Health and W ͟ ͟ ͟ ͟ ͟ ͟ ͟ ͟ ͟ ͟ ͟ ͟ ͟ ͟ ͟u

Before the World Intruded

*Conquering the Past
and Creating the Future*

A Memoir

Michele Rosenthal
YOUR LIFE AFTER TRAUMA, LLC

Cover and book design by Charles Rue Woods

International Standard Book Number (ISBN):978-0615624389
(Your Life After Trauma, LLC) 0615624383
Library of Congress Control Number: 2011940588

Printed in the United States of America
FIRST EDITION

This is a work of nonfiction. The events and experiences detailed herein are all true and have
been faithfully rendered as the author remembered them, to the best of her ability. Some
names, identities, and circumstances have changed in order to protect the privacy and/or
anonymity of the various individuals involved. Others have vetted the manuscript and confirmed its rendering of events.

For Eileen, Gary, and Bret,
who stood beside me
when I was sure joy did not exist—

And for John,
who danced beside me
as I discovered that it did.

FOREWORD
Alex Pattakos, PhD.

The philosopher and scientist Thales of Miletus, considered one of the Seven Sages of Ancient Greece, said that "getting to know yourself is extremely difficult." About a century later, another Greek philosopher by the name of Socrates espoused that "the unexamined life is not worth living." And a contemporary of Socrates, the Greek playwright Euripides, considered one of the greatest dramatists of all time, advised: "Don't attempt to heal others when you yourself are full of wounds."

The ageless wisdom of these famous Greek thinkers is alive and well in the twenty-first century. I think that most of us would agree that "getting to know ourselves" is still extremely difficult. And I suspect that while not everyone would agree that an "unexamined life is not worth living," at least in a literal sense, I have observed over the years that more and more people *are* on a quest for deeper meaning in their lives. In fact, I would say that the search for meaning has become a "megatrend" of the new millennium as people of all ages and in all walks of life are being more comfortable asking existential questions and yearn for a life that is both authentic and fulfilling, not simply for one that is grounded only—or even primarily—in pleasure or power.

At first blush, the idea of attempting "to heal others when you yourself are full of wounds" would appear to be self-evident. But I'm afraid to say that this is not the case. My personal and professional experience with the healing "arts" and allied human services professions suggests that many people enter the arena with the best of intentions but haven't done the inner work (suggested by Thales and Socrates) that is required to live up to Euripides's premise. Rather, they become human services warriors as a way to help, if not heal, themselves or to hide their "wounds" from others and many times from themselves.

This is certainly not the case of Michele Rosenthal who, in her memoir *Before the World Intruded*, demonstrates how to apply the wisdom from each of the ancient Greek thinkers mentioned here to her own life and work. To be sure, as Thales warned, confronting the struggle within is no easy task, nor is the process of discovering meaning in pain and suffering whatever their source or level of severity. On the contrary, as Michele vividly illustrates, it can be—and usually is—a formidable challenge worthy of the mighty Hercules. And since we don't always recognize that we possess the inner and outer strength to confront what life calls out to us, more often than not we find ourselves wading in thoughts and feelings that are more akin to the plight of Sisyphus, the Greek hero who was ordered by the gods to push a big rock uphill only to see it slip out of his hands at the last moment, forcing him to start over—again and again and again for eternity.

When Michele Rosenthal asked me to write a foreword to her book, it was because she recognized that both of us were passionate about life no matter what the circumstances, that we both were intrinsically motivated by the search for meaning in our lives, and that we both wanted to make a positive difference in the world by helping others reach their highest potential. This recognition, as you will discern by reading her book, did not come easy for Michele. First, she needed to recognize these qualities in herself before she would be able to see the reflection of them in others. In the process of eventually overcoming the trauma that plagued her like the big rock of Sisyphus, Michele has done much more than survive; she's thriving in a new world with a new identity—one grounded in joy, meaning, and a renewed sense of self-awareness, self-worth, self-confidence, and self-empowerment.

NOT BEING A STRANGER TO TRAUMA, I was able to resonate with Michele's ordeal in ways that only kindred spirits would understand and experience. At the same time, there are lessons to be learned from Michele that will benefit everyone. The deeper meaning of her message, in other words, offers practical guidance in the dance of life, which is something about which we all should be concerned. That is, if we really want our lives to be happy, healthy, and meaningful!

I was blessed to have had as a mentor, the world-renowned psychiatrist, Viktor Frankl, whose personal story of finding a reason to live amidst the horrors of the Nazi concentration camps has inspired millions. Dr. Frankl, I'm also very proud to say, personally urged me to write my own book about the human quest for meaning, *Prisoners of Our Thoughts.* As I consider the core principles that I introduce in my book and, importantly, how they are put into action, Michele Rosenthal has come to exemplify all of them.

First, she has learned through first-hand experience that, in all situations, no matter how desperate they may appear or actually be, that she always had (and always will have) the ultimate freedom to choose her attitude. Second, she *grew*—not just changed—into a person who has committed authentically to meaningful values and goals in *her* life; values and goals that only she can actualize and fulfill. Third, Michele learned that only she can answer for her own life by detecting the meaning at any given moment, including the meaning milestones, and by assuming personal responsibility for weaving the tapestry of her own existence. Fourth, she learned, albeit often the hard way, to avoid becoming so fixated on an intent or outcome that she actually worked against herself and the desired result. Fifth, Michele learned (and experienced) that she had/has the capacity to look at herself from a distance and gain a sense of perspective that not only helped her to cope but also to find "freedom" and possible solutions to whatever she was confronting in life. Sixth, she learned how to build her coping mechanisms for dealing with stress and change by deflecting or shifting her focus of attention from the problem (including trauma) situation to something else, preferably to something positive. And seventh, by learning how to direct her attention to something/someone else and relate to something more than herself, Michele has learned the deeper meaning of self-transcendence.

It is on this self-transcendent plane that the human spirit manifests itself and where the true essence of its resilience may play itself out in real life. Dr. Frankl learned this lesson while experiencing the horrors of the Nazi death camps and it became the hallmark of his life/work and legacy. I suspect that in Michele Rosenthal's case, she too will find out that her life/work and legacy will be guided by this meaning-centered principle.

Like all of us, Michele's life path has been like walking a labyrinth—a path of meaning to be experienced. Whether we may know it or not, when we walk the path we are never really lost even though we can never quite see where we are going. Along the path we sometimes move forward with ease and confidence; sometimes we creep ahead cautiously; sometimes we feel the need to stop and reflect; and sometimes we feel the urge to retreat. The center of the labyrinth is there but our path takes us through countless twists and turns. Sometimes we are at the heart of our life experiences, sometimes we are at a playful turn; sometimes we share our path with others, and other times we don't. No matter what, we are still on the labyrinth path. It holds all our life experiences. Indeed, in so many ways, the labyrinth is like life.

But the labyrinth is also a metaphor for what is sacred in our lives. Through its twists and turns, it holds everything we experience—our minds and emotions, our physical beings and our spirits, our losses and gains, our successes and failures, our joys and sorrows. When we walk the path inward, we carry our burdens with us. When we meditate or pray in the center, we ask for grace, forgiveness, and understanding. When we walk the path outward, we are lighter, more joyful, and ready again to take on life's challenges.

You can change without growing but you can't grow without changing. In *Before the World Intruded*, Michele Rosenthal reminds us that just because you change doesn't mean that you've grown. At the same time, she underscores that with growth, including post-traumatic growth, comes change that really means something.

CONTENTS

PART THREE: Clarity

PART FOUR: Healing

BEFORE THE WORLD INTRUDED
by Michele Rosenthal

Return me to those infant years
before I woke from sleep,

when ideas were oceans crashing,
my dreams blank shores of sand.

Transport me fast to who I was
when breath was fresh as sight,

my new parts—unfragmented—
shielded faith from unkind light.

Draw for me a figure whole,
so different from who I am.

Show me now this picture:
who I was when I began.

Prologue

When you survive a life-threatening experience you become another person justlikethat. It happens in an instant. If it's happened to you, you know exactly what I mean. One moment you are minding your own business, aware (or, if you're a child like I was, vaguely aware) of who you are and what it means to be you —and then, *Wham!*, all of a sudden that self is gone. That self is who you were 'Before'. Suddenly, it is 'After' and a new self exists. Of course, it's natural for an identity to evolve. People change all the time without distress from newborns to infants to toddlers to children to adolescents to adults. It's a gradual progression through stages. Changes occur slowly; they do not occur justlikethat.

For survivors of abuse, violence, accidents, natural disasters and combat, however, things change quickly. In a matter of moments, everything that ever felt safe, familiar, secure and normal disintegrates, to be replaced by a world that is dangerous, unpredictable, hostile and untrustworthy. The self that understood its surroundings and its place in them is suddenly thrown into question. A new figure takes control, one that is full of fear, anxiety, distrust, chaos and confusion. Many survivors go through this process and not long afterward emerge with strength and resilience. Many let go of the past, live in the present and look toward the future. I am not one of those survivors.

I was thirteen years old when I lived through an illness so rare none of my doctors had ever seen a case. For the following twenty-six years I was always looking over my shoulder, trying to go back to who I was Before, trying to make sure I was safe After. I survived in the present by being able to see what happened in the past. I verified, understood, marked consequences, guaranteed history did not repeat itself. I kept panic at bay by remaining alert. And all the while, I searched for a way to make the whole experience meaningful.

Instead of succeeding, I descended into deep depressions. I contained an enormous rage. I suffered recurring nightmares, occasional flashbacks and nightly insomnia. I existed in a state of emotional numbness, hyperarousal and hypervigilance. I avoided anything that reminded me of what I had survived. I found it difficult to concentrate. I had trouble remembering simple things. In order to relieve the enormous stress I grinned and screamed and gritted my teeth. I cried and talked and howled. I sank into silence. I saw therapists, healers, Chinese doctors, a slew of Western medicine specialists, or: I refused all medical attention. I went out every night of the week, or I collapsed into a hermetic existence. I bounced from one to another of eleven jobs in five industries in thirteen years because I was unable to decide what I wanted to spend my life doing and because sometimes, I just wasn't functional enough to work. I refused to love, and then knowingly chose to love the wrong man. In order to purge myself of the stain of one life-altering ex-perience I swung along a pendulum of extremes. Traditional therapy and popular alternative techniques didn't free me. I vacillated between feeling a little better and feeling a lot worse, going through the motions of a young woman's life and suffering dire new inexplicable physical ailments or complete emotional meltdowns.

And then something in me snapped. Or, something decided it desperately wanted to be free. Finally, I couldn't bear to live in the Before/After gap. I decided to haul myself out. It all began with the need to put into some chronological order the many fragments I carried of my past. I wanted to understand what had happened to me, plus how I had become the lost woman I was. When I started writing this book I was physically debilitated by stress symptoms and in a dark fog of emotional and mental disturbance. As I wrote, however, circumstances began to change. This is the story of how I finally found freedom from horrific memories, terror, fear, anxiety, chaos, confusion and powerlessness. This is the story of how I found myself 'Now', and the very unexpected way it happened.

PART ONE:

SHOCK

Before the World Intruded

In the summer of 1981, I was thirteen years old. My brother, Bret, was ten. At the end of June we flew with our parents to Arizona where we picked up a twenty-six-foot Winnebago that became our home for the next four weeks. Our route took us all over the West, from Phoenix to Flagstaff, across the Mojave Desert, through Indian reservations, the Grand Canyon, all the way up to Lake Tahoe, California, from where we drove 607 miles down the California coast on Route 1, past Big Sur, through Los Angeles, to San Diego.

We drove for hours each day across deserts and long spans of highway. We spent nights in recreation vehicle campgrounds hooking and then unhooking electricity wires and sewage hoses. We ate microwave pizzas and salvaged watermelons that exploded on the floor every time my father took a sharp turn. By day, we felt the requisite awe in the face of what my mother called "intimacy with a natural phenomenon." We stood in a very still row to see the sun set over the Painted Desert. We rode horses around the North Rim of the Grand Canyon while my father, overloaded by a still camera slung over one shoulder and a moving camera over the other, tried to capture the beauty of the landscape. We climbed cave dwellings at Montezuma, shouting encouragement to help Bret overcome his fear of heights.

We were making our way across the western end of America in the tight bubble only a happy family can make. We howled at my father's practical jokes. We giggled as we watched my mother, five foot two, one hundred ten pounds, try to drive the Winnebago down the steepest part of Big Sur without the great vehicle running away from her on the curves. We groaned collectively on our way to Silverado when the camper broke down, again, and we had to hitch-hike to the nearest service station, all of us squeezing into the backseat of a woman's tiny brown sedan.

When we arrived at Lake Tahoe, the air was cold and smooth and crisp. At our forest campground in the morning, fir trees emitted a damp, piney smell and the sun crept through the branches, spattering the dark forest floor with a shy light. We decided to go white-water rafting. I pulled on my green-and-white-striped racing tank and studied the map to see the river's route as it twisted through the High Sierra.

We shoved off, my father in the back of the raft, providing a good rudder, while I swooped my paddle through the current to bring us closer to shore or farther out into the middle of the river. We maneuvered around other rafters. We hit up against a sandbar. At times, the river was calm and we floated in the July sunshine as serenely as a lily pad. At other times, the river moved so swiftly and strongly, water climbed over the sides until we were all hip deep in it. The river, as we got farther downstream, became chaotic.

"How much farther do we have to go?" my mother asked.

My father promised to be careful, and then pretended to lose his paddle in a farcical pantomime. Bret and I laughed hysterically. Mom bit her lip and tightened her hold on the raft until her knuckles turned white.

We came to a whirlpool that had to be navigated in

order to slip over the smooth edge of a rock wall and down into a calm pool near the base camp. The first time around, we missed the edge and the whirlpool delivered us back upstream. Mom clung to the raft and we whirled around again and again. More water sloshed over the sides of the raft. The coolness of the river slipped around my thighs and between my knees while I knelt on the raft's rubber floor.

Here's where the story breaks down. I have a predisposition for bladder infections and had been warned not to sit in a wet bathing suit. But it had been a whole year since my last infection, and that was the furthest thing from my mind when the water reached four inches in the raft and I was kneeling in it for hours. There were no worries on that July day. Everything in our world was under control. We were not being vigilant.

And that, of course, is exactly when the world intrudes.

One Pink Pill

We returned to Scarsdale from our Western vacation and settled back into New York life. I spent days at the municipal pool with my friends rating our efforts on the high dive. We visited each other's houses and planned how to restyle our hair for the start of school in a month. The summer was lazily moving toward its conclusion when I felt the familiar twinge and burn of a bladder infection. My pediatrician was on vacation, so we met with the covering doctor. He listened to my complaints, took a culture, confirmed the infection, and prescribed the antibiotic Septra. Each morning I took the large pink pill with a big glass of cranberry juice and waited for things to get better.

But things didn't get better. Within a few days of taking the first pill I was lethargic, tired and had an overwhelming sense of something not being right in my body. A migraine headache settled into residence. Soon, my eyes became completely bloodshot and sensitive to light. We went back to the doctor. He sent us back home. When the symptoms worsened, we made the rounds to other doctors: allergists and dermatologists and opthalmologists. My mother asked about the large pink pill. *Nothing to worry about,* everyone told her. *Your daughter has a virus; that's all. Go home,* they all agreed. *Get some sleep.*

After six days of this, two things happened: a rash erupted all over my body and two tiny blisters appeared on my bottom lip. That night, my body too itchy and my head too painful for sleep, I lay in bed in my darkened room. My mother bathed me in cool baths and laid chilled washcloths all over my torso and limbs. I listened to the summer sounds of our suburban neighborhood, to the children playing in the street, to the cicadas whirring in the humid August air. My mother wanted to spend the night in my room but I was restless and agitated and somewhere around 2 a.m. asked her to leave. Minute by painful minute I watched the early morning hours flip by on the illuminated clock beside my bed. I did not sleep at all.

Immediately the next morning my parents took me back to the covering pediatrician. We showed him the small bubbles on my mouth. We showed him the rash. We told him I hadn't slept. We told him I was in pain. We asked for help and waited for him to offer up a diagnosis. He examined me and then we were ushered into his office, where he sat surrounded by brown leather and oak.

Hands clasped on top of his large, paper-filled desk, he

surveyed us in silence.

Finally he shrugged, shook his head, and said, "I don't know what this is."

We stared at him in disbelief.

"I think you have two choices," he continued. "We can wait and see how things develop over the next couple of days, or you can go to the hospital today."

I'm sure he said more than that. I'm sure there was a medical discussion I don't remember because the word *hospital* escaped into the air like a powerful fume and I didn't hear anything after that. I realized something might be seriously wrong and way beyond the realm of family pediatrics. I realized I was not completely safe. Maybe I don't recall the rest of the doctor's conversation because I was lost in the chaos forming in my own head, the phrase "I don't know" beginning the slow unraveling of order.

The office where we sat was dark and frightening and depressing. Outside the windows, however, it was a bright, sunny August morning—my favorite time of year in my favorite season, when the smell of the bushes on our front lawn perfumed the entire neighborhood. Outside that blue and white medical building on Central Avenue in Hartsdale, New York, the sky was bright aqua, shiny, nearly cloudless. Traffic sped by. Birds sang. Children everywhere enjoyed the final days of summer vacation.

After a moment of drifting along in the implications of this doctor's impotence, I pressed my back firmly into the chair. I had watched my parents remain calm in the face of other crises; I knew what to do. Keep your breath even. Deal with the moment. Don't speculate on the future. Most of all, hold yourself together in body and mind so the right decisions can be made. I didn't feel actively frightened. Instead, I felt an unnatural calm. I understood that my parents and

I were essentially without guidance.

My focus receded from the room. It was clear which of the doctor's choices to pick.

WITHIN TWO HOURS MY PARENTS, Bret and I were cruising along the Cross County Parkway toward New York-Presbyterian Hospital in Manhattan. I was admitted but no doctor could figure out what was wrong. It wasn't until the end of the day, when a young, high-profile dermatologist came onto the case that anyone began to suspect I might be having a very rare allergic reaction to the antibiotic I was taking for the bladder infection.

A tall, imposing figure with a sharp stare, loud voice, and boisterous laugh, Dr. Marc Grossman had wiry brown hair that framed a large face with large features. While he cheerfully admitted he'd never seen a case of Stevens-Johnson Syndrome (SJS), he thought I fit the profile for this unusual illness.

"Stevens-Johnson Syndrome is rare. Recently, I read an article about it and I think. . . . I think that might be what's happening here. There's not much we're going to be able to do to help you. But we'll do our best to make you comfortable as the illness takes its course. Your body is going to get rid of the medication by sending it out through your skin."

We felt a little bit of security in the way Dr. Grossman's body language filled up the room, the way his self-confidence overshadowed the collective ignorance of the other doctors who remained baffled. Dr. Grossman gave us a name for the pain. In return we gave him our undivided allegiance and attention.

"The first thing to do," he said, "is stop taking those pink pills."

Soon, blisters began forming all over my body and the

doctor warned us to be prepared. "Things'll get worse before they get better!" he announced each day when we told him of some frightening new development.

The staff remained woefully behind in predicting or slowing the illness's progression. Ultimately, my parents became the primary managers of my care. My mother directed the staff and devised creative ways to get things done. To move me from one position to another, or from one bed to another, my mother was always the one figuring out how to do the impossible with the least amount of pain. Meanwhile, my father corralled doctors, located medications, and tracked down informational leads. My parents didn't panic. They didn't cry. They didn't wail, moan, carry on, or wring their hands—at least not in front of me. Instead, they got to work and became my advocates and nurses, the cheerleaders whose voices would guide my way.

My mother set up a cot in my room so she could sleep beside my bed. That first night my father went home, but on the second night Bret moved into a friend's house and my father set up a second cot beside my mother. I was taking massive doses of Prednisone and Benadryl in an attempt to stop the allergy from escalating. My parents met with doctors and hired nurses to care for me around the clock. Specialists from all over the hospital came to examine me.

I lay in bed with my eyes closed. The headache had become so intense that even the smallest noise was too much. My father bought a little white clock radio with a neon blue display and put it on the metal shelf above my bed. The idea was that music would soothe and distract me, but the sound of drums and synthesizers and voices straining through the tiny speaker was too much for me to bear.

The blisters on my lips and torso continued to develop, but they were small, the size of chicken pox, an illness of which I had fond memories since Bret and I had it together and spent most of our days driving Mom crazy by jumping on the beds and blowing up balloons we let fly around the room as we doubled over with laughter.

I lay in my hospital bed thinking these little blisters and this big headache were as bad as things would get. I was wrong.

The Face in the Mirror

By the time I walked through the automatic doors of the hospital, I had become an automaton. I was not the actor; I was being acted upon. The vague unease over my lack of safety became a passive constant and, once in the hospital, I became constantly passive. I reclined on the bed and the world revolved around me. Parents and doctors and nurses pushed the day through its relentless hours while I watched, while I listened, while I did not engage.

In the middle of the second afternoon I passed a mirror mounted on the wall next to the bathroom in my room. I knew my unwashed hair appeared matted from being smashed against the pillow. I knew that except for a few strands, all my hair was pulled away from my face with a barrette, princess style. I knew I would look tired from not having slept. Still, I turned reflexively when the mirror came into view.

I had been judging my status from the expressions of those around me. Nurses bustled. Doctors noted. My parents smiled. People were cheerful and matter-of-fact.

No face registered disgust or horror. No eyes looked repulsed or terrified. It had not occurred to me my face would elicit those reactions. But when I looked in the mirror, those things were what I felt.

My lips were so swollen they seemed to take up the entire bottom half of my face. They were a deep, crimson red, scabbed, bubbled, and bleeding. They'd felt uncomfortable; I had begun drinking through a straw because I could not work my lips around the rim of a cup. But it had not occurred to me that the discomfort might make me appear significantly changed.

My eyes, so deeply brown the pupils are almost invisible, had always been the focus of my face. But now my features shrank in relation to the mouth grown to disproportionate size. My face itself had become slightly swollen, the skin beginning to stretch with subcutaneous fluid. My swollen eyes pulled uncomfortably at the corners. The only familiar feature was the eyeballs themselves, two familiar beads looking out in shock.

I took a good look at the lips. I examined the skin around the eyes. I searched the pupils for an anchor to who I was. Yes, I could see her. But now the body existed between her and me.

I went into the bathroom and closed the door. When I came out I saw that someone had covered the mirror with a surgical gown.

Behold the Zebra!

In his memoir, *One Hundred Days: My Unexpected Journey from Doctor to Patient,* Dr. David Biro describes the medical profession's excitement at finding a zebra—an unusual medical condition:

> *Doctors . . . love a good zebra. . . .Patients with rare, exotic diseases. . . . We crowd around to see them, touch them, photograph them. We put them on display at conferences. We write their stories in journals. We do all this, I suspect, because they reawaken the spirit that first pushed us into medicine: a fascination with the human body, its incredible achievements and its terrifying failings.*

I was an exciting zebra. New York-Presbyterian Hospital is a world-renowned facility, yet no one at the hospital had ever seen such an illness, much less had the opportunity to monitor its development. Throughout the day professionals in all areas of medicine came to view my case. Doctors, interns, and residents met in groups to discuss my symptoms. Internists, dermatologists, and opthalmologists pried, analyzed, and noted particular presentations of my illness. Some spoke to me; others just observed. They came while I was resting; they came during various procedures. They stood silently in corners; they huddled in groups at the foot of my bed while I gritted my teeth, closed my eyes, and let my naked, deformed body be studied. My case was thoroughly documented and, in the year to come, written up and presented.

I accepted the constant flow of curious spectators. They weren't looking at me; they were just looking at a body. While physicians poked and prodded and endlessly examined me, I resigned myself to the role of freak du jour. I lay on my back, exposed, immobilized by pain and fear, and allowed myself to be ogled. As each new round of faces entered my room, I held myself still and played the model patient.

It was an intern with a camera who finally overcrowded the zoo. After enduring a long day of chatty gawkers and painful procedures, I was resting in the late afternoon when a tall, frizzy-haired woman in her thirties, wearing a white lab coat, came bustling in to measure, document, and record the hugeness of the blisters. SJS blisters become bullae: blisters measuring about 4 x 6 inches each, then joining together so that, for example, my entire torso from navel to neck was one large sac of liquid that continued to grow as it crept toward both my left and right side and threatened to roll around in an effort to join its kin on my back.

I learned that if I didn't move, the blisters sometimes combined at a slower rate. I trained myself to lie still as a corpse. To let the breath flow in and out, but to let that be the only movement. Even so, that afternoon the bulla's liquid would not stop inching upward. It began at my belly button and slowly crept from my stomach toward the base of my neck. At first I accepted the movement as normal, but then, as the bulla negotiated over my breasts, an unmitigated terror grew. I became frightened that the bulla would not stop but would creep up over my chin to cover my mouth.

"Do something!" I yelled at my mother. "I'm going to be smothered!"

My mother, in her usual calm way, stood beside the bed and tried to reason with me. Her words, however, were meaningless against the sensation of the bulla's movement below my skin. Again I screamed and begged her to lance the blister before I suffocated. Again she reminded me, "Blisters can only go where there is a continuous surface. Your mouth is open. Don't worry. You're safe."

Reasoning was useless. I became hysterical. In the end, my mother placed her hand below my chin and promised to protect me. I sank back into an exhausted state of mute despair. Shortly afterward, when the intern showed up and asked permission to photograph, my mother refused. The doctor, however, would not be denied. She marched off down the hall and sent the Chief of Staff to negotiate. "Mrs. Rosenthal, I'm very sorry, but this is a teaching hospital; photographs are needed for research and later lessons."

"Michele has had a very hard day."

"This will only take a few minutes."

"She needs to rest."

"This needs to be done."

"But—"

"I'm not asking." He motioned to the internist.

The frizzy-haired doctor brusquely set up her equipment. She had a still camera and a long metal chain she used to measure each bulla. She took an endless number of pictures, asking me to roll my head this way and that. Her bulb flashed until my light-sensitive eyes, already beginning to blister beneath the lids, ached with the burst of each strobe. I tried to think about the benefits these photos would bring other people. I did everything I could to be a good patient—and then I burst into tears.

My mother hustled her out of the room. After that, there were no more group rounds, no more photo sessions, and no educational discussions dissecting my latest symptoms. The freak show was over. My father stood like a sentry outside the door to my room, refusing access to any group who came by on rounds. Eventually, we were left alone.

Every morning, we asked, *Is this the worst it will be?* And Dr. Grossman would deflect the question, often making a joke designed to elicit my mother's blush and fill the room with his loud and raucous guffaws before he ducked out with the promise to return. Each day more blisters appeared, more infections threatened, more skin hung off and sloughed off and stuck to the bed, the sheets, anything that touched me. My room was placed in quarantine. I could receive no visitors, and anyone entering the room had to wear a cap, mask, and gown. Each day, as my body was racked with new outbreaks and wept with old ones, we thought, *It can't get any worse.* And yet it did. One morning, my feet swelled beneath my calloused soles; the next, my hands blistered so it looked like I was wearing a pair of latex gloves. The inside of my eyelids erupted. My mouth and throat filled with sores that brought on a frenzy of the staff asking, *What should we do? What should we do?*

The Bed

The illness took off with surprising speed. Blisters everywhere enlarged to bullae. I was bedridden, barely able to move, and then came the day when it was determined I had to be moved: The bullae needed a different environment in which to evolve. The delicacy of my skin required the kind of bed used for burn patients.

There was a brief discussion in which it was proposed I be moved to the premier burn unit of another hospital.

"No. Absolutely not," my mother told the ring of physicians around her. "It would be too painful."

"Mrs.—" My mother cut the doctor off.

"And I don't want her surrounded by burn patients. She's a thirteen year old child. And she is not a burn patient. She has an illness that needs burn protocol. That's entirely different. I want her in her own private room."

"We'll bring a burn-unit bed here," my father added. "We'll hire burn-unit nurses. We can turn this room into its own burn unit."

Dr. Grossman supported my parents. He showed them an article he'd read about an advanced technology burn bed just hitting the market. It was so new no local hospital had even acquired one.

For the next twenty-four hours my father researched and tracked down resources. He and my mother interviewed and hired burn unit nurses. My father located one of the new burn beds in New Jersey.

"You'll never get it here, tomorrow's Labor Day," Dr. Grossman said.

"It'll be here," my father replied and disappeared to make more phone calls.

When it arrived the next day, the new bed was twice the width and about three feet longer than the regular hospital bed. It had blue Fiberglass sides, about two feet high and there was a long metal bar overhead. In concept it was like a waterbed, with an enormous plastic sack filled with silicon beads. A plastic sheet, punctured by thousands of tiny pinholes through which air could circulate, stretched to all four corners of the square, steel frame. The bed was high up off the ground, like a tub sitting on top of a metal square in which there was a fan that, when switched on, made the silicon beads float, thereby rendering me weightless. The weightlessness would significantly reduce the pain of anything pressing against my blistered skin. The constant circulation of air would keep my skin dry and help reduce the risk of infection.

The problem, after the bed was installed and tested and the cots moved and my own bed wheeled aside, was how to move a patient who cannot be touched. I was in too much pain to move myself, and no one could pick me up because there was no unaffected skin onto which they could hold. In the end, a cranelike hydraulic lift was brought in. My parents, two nurses and two orderlies grasped the edges of my bedsheet and lifted me—as I screamed and howled from the pressure of fabric against my skin—so that the lift's harness could be slung below me. I was settled into it and then the lift was jerkily cranked up, inch by excruciating inch. My parents coached and encouraged while I swung and bounced above one bed and across and down onto the other.

"Mommy, help me!" I cried out in pain. My parents crooned and soothed until finally I was deposited, naked, exhausted, and pain-ravaged, on the silicon-buoyed sheet.

When the crane had been hauled away and the orderlies dismissed, a switch on the bed was thrown; in a terrifying instant the pressure beneath my back gave way and I was floating in this new bed that would be my prison for the next two weeks.

Pain

Once it burst on the scene, my scream would not be denied. It hung around the edges of my mouth, waiting. It knocked against my teeth, begging to be let out. In each situation heightening the level of pain, the scream demanded the catharsis of delivering that pain from my body. Each utterance birthed a part of my horror away from me and into the room, where it ricocheted off the ceiling and walls until it crashed to the ground in a great flaming ball of pain.

It's hard to remember all the details you'd like to when you're doped up on Demerol and Morphine. I tried, diligently, to be aware of minutiae and the chronology of things. But sometimes I only succeeded in generalities: the movement of shadows across the happy family photos taped to the wall; the placement of my mother, in one moment at the window, pensively contemplating the Hudson River, in another moment, in the chair beside my bed. But how long was she at the window? One minute? An hour? How long did she sit in the chair, head bent over a canvas, needlepointing in the soft light of a single lamp?

In the end I most clearly remember things that made the largest impression. Not necessarily the events you'd expect, but those most charged with meaning. And also, idiosyncratic moments, like the distance between my mother's face and mine (about six inches), how loudly I was screaming (enough for the walls to echo with my misery), how dim the room was in the middle of the day (gray, despite the suggestion of sun outside the single window), my father's presence by my side (strong, although I don't remember him saying a word), my favorite nurse's eyes (big, brown, liquid, with a thick mascara fringe above the surgical mask, below the cap).

When you're frightened, it's hard to remember all the physical details. But the emotional details—those incidents that your soul, however unwillingly, recorded—remain eternally clear: Terror. Chaos. Pain. Fear. In my body, every cell registered, memorized, and retained what scarred it in those moments.

By the end of the first week I was covered, head to toe, inside and out, with bullae. I could not swallow. I could not move. I was terrified and at the same time too tired to exert any energy on fear.

One morning the internist threatened to insert a feeding tube. When my mother resisted the doctor agreed to give her until that afternoon to find an alternative. My weight was dropping quickly. I had entered the hospital at five foot five, weighing 110 pounds. I had lost ten pounds and was now unable to chew any food. The medical staff was worried, especially since the IV that had been feeding me would soon need to be removed. My mother left me in the care of Gayle, my favorite nurse, and exited the room.

She returned an hour later, after a short trip and a raid on the supply closet at the end of the hall. In one hand my mother carried an enormous and fat syringe without a needle; in the other, a vanilla milkshake my father had procured from McDonald's.

"This is the plan," she said. "I'm going to fill the syringe with shake. All you have to do is open your mouth. Okay?"

I looked at her skeptically.

"Do not swallow. Do not move. Just let the shake slip down your throat." She demonstrated by tipping her head back and pumping the syringe so the white liquid disappeared into her mouth.

The first squirt of shake into my mouth did not go down. A reflexive gag sent it dribbling out both sides of my mouth. Gayle cautiously patted my face with gauze. My mother tried again; I gagged; Gayle patted. And again, until with practice, I suppressed the reflex. If I held myself very still and concentrated on the grainy sensation of the shake floating down my throat, I could resist the feeling I was choking. If I refused the urge to taste, to swallow—to, in any way, participate in this potential pleasure—I could let the liquid roll in a cool path toward my stomach.

It was slow going, but forty-five minutes, many breaks, and several syringefuls later, I had ingested about a quarter of the shake. By the time the doctor returned for afternoon rounds, I had gotten almost the whole thing down. My mother, poised over my bed with syringe in hand, regarded her triumphantly. The doctor looked surprised and bemused. Then she shook her head and offered a short, uncharacteristic laugh.

"You win," she said. "But she'll need four shakes a day."

"We'll do it," my mother answered and drew another 50cc into the syringe.

AS THE DAYS MOVED FORWARD we learned there are procedures and protocols in the treatment of burn patients. For example, I needed to be turned every few hours to let different patches of skin breathe. It seemed I was constantly being rolled over, treated, and disinfected. Dead skin was ripped off; raw skin was cleansed. Every moment brought some excruciating pain and so I screamed and cried and begged to be left alone, and when that didn't happen I begged for more Demerol, more Morphine, less pain.

By my ninth day in the hospital my entire body was

raw and exposed. The doctors decided the risk of infection was so great it called for drastic measures. A special disinfectant foam was procured from the burn unit; it sprayed bright orange in a thin stream from a white aerosol can. Nurses stood on either side of the bed, cans raised, fingers poised over the nozzles. They worked as a team, starting at my feet and moving upward to spread the foam which fluffed up like shaving cream to cover a large area. On contact with my skin it felt like raging fire.

We had been warned it would take nineteen seconds for the fiery feeling to dissipate. With each spray my mother counted and I tried to focus on the numbers. The nurses covered my feet with the stuff while I screamed in agony and begged them to stop. Then they moved up to my legs. I thrashed in the bed. The burning enveloped my ankles, moving up from my shins toward the tops of my thighs. More Demerol was added to the IV and I was given extra Morphine. Still, nothing quelled the pain.

"Make it stop! Make it stop!" I panted and screamed.

"This will ensure you don't get an infection," my mother explained again. "Let's think about the pierced earrings you're going to buy when we get home."

This had become a dynamic strategy for my mother: In moments of excruciating pain she and I would play a game of bartering. She would say, "If you can bear this, you can have anything you want. What do you choose?"

"I can have anything?"

"Yes."

"Anything . . . ?"

"Anything."

And then I'd ask for something I'd been wanting and she and my father had been refusing for months.

In this way, I got them to agree to let me pierce my ears.

A few days later, I finagled a phone extension in my bedroom. And then, on a day when things were truly awful, I got them to agree to give me my own phone line.

On this day, however, the game did not work. This pain was too intense. Because of the way it spread from one location to another, I could not localize it in my mind and so compartmentalize it in experience. I imagined my whole body feeling on fire, and the idea made me feel insane. I simply could not take it. My mother knew.

"You're going to have to stop this," she said.

The doctors argued.

"Put the cans away," she said firmly.

They backed off.

The nurses cleansed the foam from my legs.

I cried until the pain became more manageable, and then my dialect for suffering switched to a whimper before I fell into an exhausted, defeated sleep.

No Words

Days passed in a cycle of pain and release. Powerless, I laid immobilized flat on my back. A few times a day a team of nurses rolled me over and separated skin stuck to the sheet. When the inside of my eyelids erupted in blisters my father bought out the hospital's supply and then scoured the city for a medicated cream the opthalmologist thought might stop my corneas from being damaged. The cream was so thick and opaque that once it was administered, I couldn't see through it. The room blurred and, instead of shapes, I could only discern varying degrees of light.

I remember my father pulling up a chair beside the bed and reading to me. I liked the diversion, plus the sound of his voice close by, which made me feel secure.

Two weeks after I was admitted blisters stopped erupting and raw skin began to dry up and flake off. Instead of being in pain, I was in an itching frenzy as the skin repaired itself. The burn bed was removed. I no longer had to drink from a syringe or a straw. McDonald's shakes were supplemented by meals my mother cooked on a small stove in the nurses' kitchen. My father wheeled a tray to my bed, and we set up fierce games of ten-card gin so that I was too busy to scratch and pull at my skin.

Once healing began the momentum built daily. As we neared our third week in the hospital, a day was chosen for me to be released.

My mother felt it was important for me to speak to the hospital psychiatrist before I went home. I vehemently opposed the idea.

"I just want to go home," I insisted as my mother tossed a fresh bowl of fettuccine alfredo she'd made down the hall.

"I think it would be a good idea for you to talk about what happened," she answered. "I want you to give it a try."

"I can't talk about it."

"Sure you can."

"No, I can't."

"Why not?"

"Because I don't want to."

"If you don't like it, you won't have to do it again." My mother handed me the bowl and a fork. Fettuccine al fredo was one of my favorites of my mother's dishes and I had requested it. This was my second day back on real food. The smell of the sauce and the sensation of the pasta gliding over my tongue and down my throat were indescribably delicious.

"There aren't words to express any of it," I said.

"It would still be good for you to try."

I reached for a vanilla shake and said what any self-respecting teenager would: "Well, you can tell the shrink to come, but I won't talk to her."

The psychiatrist showed up the afternoon before my release from the hospital. Relatively short, she had shoulder-length light brown hair and a square figure. She wore a dark suit with clear stockings and a white blouse. She sat in a vinyl chair by the side of my bed and greeted me with a chipper expectancy.

"Hello, Michele."

I glanced at her and looked away.

"How are you today?"

I stared across the room at the television suspended from the wall.

"How are you feeling?"

"Fine."

"You're going home tomorrow."

"Yes."

"I thought it would be good if we talked for a little while."

"There's nothing to talk about."

Tom and Jerry chased each other across the screen. I kept my eyes on the cartoon while the doctor addressed my profile.

"Well, you just experienced something very difficult, something pretty scary."

"Yeah."

"Tell me how you feel about that."

"I don't feel anything."

"I know it's difficult, but try."

"I'm fine."

"You must feel something."

"I feel relieved I'm going home. There's nothing else to say."

"I think there's probably a lot to say."

When I didn't respond, she tried a different tack.

"Are you excited to be going home?"

"Yes."

"What are you most looking forward to doing when you get there?"

"Being left alone."

She kept trying, but I did not tell her how drastically I felt changed. I would not say out loud that I was trying to suppress the memory of a pain so intense it defied words. I could not explain that I was struggling not to be overwhelmed by a staggering number of new fears and feelings, nor even the latest fear: that I had survived the physical onslaught only to be undone by the emotions in its wake.

While the psychiatrist continued to speak, Tom and Jerry ended their battle and I clicked the remote until I found Scooby-Doo slouching his way through a haunted house. Finally, she ceased talking and together we watched the dog and gang solve another ghost-filled mystery until her allotted time had elapsed and she left the room.

The New Girl

By the time I left the hospital it seemed important never to speak about the experience to anyone. I was told I would make a full recovery. Despite some scarring in my eyes and on my legs and wrists, there would be no evidence of my illness. I was released in the middle of September on a bright and shiny day. My parents and I said good-bye to the staff while an orderly wheeled me from my room to the hospital entrance. As we exited the building and came out into the sun I had two overwhelming thoughts: First, given my behavior in certain moments, I did not deserve to survive. Second, now I must do something to make my survival worthwhile. I didn't know what to do or how to think the problem through. I pushed the thought away and climbed into the car.

My father left straight from the hospital on a long-delayed business trip. While my mother drove home I reclined in the backseat of the car and simply watched the familiar highway sights go by. The brown brick apartment buildings of Riverside Heights looked the same. The sign to the Bronx Zoo was unaltered. The highway curved as it always had and passed by familiar ponds and stretched over the usual bridges. Large maple trees still hung over certain patches of road, and the yellow stoplight still blinked at the exit for Tuckahoe Road.

My bedroom at 79 Carman Road looked the same as it had since I was two: pink and white gingham wallpaper, pink carpet, white furniture, twin double beds with floral bedspreads, white ruffles. A view down the perpendicular Johnson Road still stretched beneath a canopy of maple trees. I recognized our sleepy, suburban town thirty miles north of New York City.

What I didn't recognize was my body in the bathtub I'd been splashing in my whole life. Down to ninety-two pounds, I weakly climbed into the white porcelain and lowered myself into hot water. I watched my skin turn varying shades of red, some patches darker or lighter than others, some patches white, depending upon where the skin had been ripped, or torn, or scratched off before it was ready to release. I bathed with the soap the doctor suggested for sensitive skin. The simple motions of getting into the bath and lathering a washcloth left me dizzy and faint. I called out to my mother in the adjoining room. She came in and took over.

My care had been exceptional. I would later learn that for many SJS victims, the skin changes color. I did not look like a burn victim. The aftereffects were subtle. All of my freckles had duplicated themselves, although not exactly on target. Where there was one freckle, now there was the original, plus a shadow where the pigmentation had missed its mark. Where the skin had ripped off prematurely, now there were irregular coffee-colored stains on my legs and wrists. Still, I looked like myself overall: fair-skinned, deep brown eyes, rosy lips. Something about the eyes, however, had changed. When I looked into them I didn't see myself, I saw her—the freak, the survivor, the zebra.

I didn't know how to relate to this other person. We were now both trapped in the same body and I didn't know how to divvy the responsibilities, or when either should defer to the other. I didn't know how to be my old self with her watching, or how to be entirely her new self. I didn't know how this girl would speak or act or what she would care about. I didn't know how to escape her, either. She moved like a shadow behind and beside me.

Rather than figure out how to meld us together, I denied her right to exist. I wanted the old me back. I concentrated on impersonating who I was before rather than stepping into this new self I didn't exactly understand. I was cheerful. I laughed. I smiled. I joked. I spent those first recuperative weeks at home learning to deny any thoughts about what had happened. I convalesced. I read. I studied the assignments my mother went to my school to pick up. I didn't think. I didn't reflect. I sat in bed eating the hot croissants with melting butter my mother brought each morning to help me regain weight. I knew that I would make a full recovery physically, but I now lived in a world of medical mistakes, the body's betrayals, and life-threatening surprises. The present no longer felt safe, but full of possible transformations I was powerless to predict or intercept.

In order to suppress all of that, I proceeded as if nothing out of the ordinary had occurred. I didn't want to admit that a substantial part of my soul had been irrevocably altered. I didn't want to admit that even in memory, the terror and pain made me feel near to crazy. Or that sometimes, thoughts so threatened to overwhelm me I imagined the utterance of a single word, the allowance of a single tear, would bring about such a total destruction of sanity I would need to be sedated, bundled into a straitjacket, and admitted to the psychiatric ward. More than anything, I didn't want to reveal that although I felt secure at home, surrounded by the love of my parents and Bret, when I looked in the mirror, I did not recognize the new girl who looked back.

Disconnection

It took six weeks for my body to recover enough weight and stamina for me to return to school. I went back around Halloween and joined my eighth grade class as if nothing had happened. My friends were friendly but a little distant. Although I had been connected to a large group of friends before my illness, while I was out of school alliances had shifted. I was on the outside of the new groups that had formed.

None of that mattered to me. I walked through the halls of Scarsdale Junior High School quietly trying to choke off a new, paranoid self beginning to lurk around the edges of my mind. Self-preservation became key; introversion and secrecy emerged as the first necessary steps to survival. Friendships didn't seem that important while my mind grasped the extent of experience and strove to protect and support the newly fragile soul.

I dove back into my studies. I conjugated French verbs, and moved x and y from one side of an equal sign to the other. I wrote cinquains in my English class and long poems about the sea. I refused to speak about what had happened in the hospital, even with my family. I told no one that my anxiety kept me up at night, or that fragments of the past just wouldn't stop flitting through my mind. Once again I lay in the dark for hours watching the minutes flip by on the clock. While the new friends I made at school worried about boys and clothes, I refused to worry about what to do with my memories. Methodically I pushed them as far down inside me as they would go.

Several years passed before I tried to tell the story of my illness to a friend. Even then, it didn't come out right. I first had to take a step back. I had to recede from the scene, divorcing myself from the immediate moment so my stomach didn't knot, so my mouth didn't inexplicably lose the ability to form words. So my brain didn't shut down and turn this woman with a wide vocabulary into a stumbling and stuttering idiot groping for language. Everything I said sounded at once melodramatic and exaggeratedly averse to pity. Too many fragments of scenes existed, too many slices of emotions bobbed unmoored in my mind. I didn't trust the story or myself, so I eliminated the grotesque and lurid, the deeply personal and spiritual, all the details that make a story communicable, until there was nothing left except to say, *It was pretty bad.*

For years I had to look away from my audience to tell the story, as if they'd see in me emotions I'd rather hide; as if I'd see in them reactions I'd rather hide from. I could not speak directly about the subject, so I talked in vague generalities. I got cavalier and shrugged and laughed and talked too fast and switched the topic as soon as possible.

Later a lover asked searchingly in the middle of the night and I tried again. It was easier in the dark. I told the story succinctly, as monotone as possible. Quickly. Invisibly. The sequence of events became somewhat coherent. In the dark he couldn't see the tremor the memory caused in me. He kissed and caressed me and murmured empathies. In his arms I grew bold. I added a little more detail. The shudder of memory quelled. After a while, I attempted to view the scenes as he must, with an outsider's distance. With a matter-of-fact attitude I gave more solid details with less gravity, and then a disturbing thing happened: The more details I gave, the more proud I became that I had survived, the more defiant I felt, the more heroic I became. I was embarrassed. How could someone talk about a life-threatening experience and feel *proud?*

Something was getting lost in translation from my interior life to the exterior world. I stopped trying to tell the story. If I had to, I said only, *I had Stevens-Johnson Syndrome.* No one knew what that meant.

Courage Is a Choice

Although I never told anyone, there was one experience during my illness that haunted me more than any other. It was the reason for my silence, my severed selves, my chaos, fear, and confusion. It was the reason I kept looking back, and also why I could not move forward. More than the others, I couldn't let this enormous memory go.

By the tenth day in the hospital, we had a routine: Three times a day a team of nurses arrived to turn me over. I was rolled from my back to my side and onto my back again after the wounds and the bed had been cleaned. When my skin adhered to the plastic sheet, syringes of water were squirted along the base of the connection in order to loosen the bond between skin and plastic. Sometimes the body reclaimed the flesh; other times, the bed refused to relinquish its hold.

When we first began these procedures, I was stoic and brave. I gnashed my teeth. I cried. I felt the pain, refuted it, refused it. I accepted the challenge without any idea the pain would be victorious.

And then, one day, it was.

The procedure began normally enough. My entire back and right leg adhered to the bed. It was slow going with the water, and it wasn't working. Each spot pried from the bed ripped off the skin. In a torrent of shrieks and tears and screams, I begged for the process to be halted. I approached a place of pain beyond where I had ever been, one that made me feel a frenzy of insanity. For the first time I thought I might not have the capacity to endure. The procedure continued, the pain increased, and then, in one of those moments of unexpected, unreal clarity, the thought suddenly occurred to me that I didn't have to endure. I had a choice.

The connection between my body and me suddenly severed.

I felt a creeping sensation of peace. The procedure continued, but I no longer cared about the body's limbs or bones, its tearing flesh, its bleeding sores. I no longer worried about its lips that sprayed a fountain of blood, or the hands clawing each other to scratch the itch of ruptured skin, or the back welded to the mattress. The pain continued but it was no longer mine.

And then I knew I had an even bigger choice: I was not required to survive. I could free myself by choosing not to fight for my life. I could choose to surrender. I could let myself die.

My body relaxed completely. All energy seemed to flow one way down my arms and legs and out of me entirely. I no longer felt the weight of my limbs or the sensation of pain. Suddenly, I felt myself rising upward, out of my body. There I lay, long, lean, and naked in the bed, and here I was, light, buoyant, and free in the air above me, aware of the body below yet mesmerized by the pull of a dark tunnel near the ceiling. The darkness seemed to stretch infinitely before me and was ringed with a bright, white light.

In a state of utter peace, I followed the impulse to float into the tunnel's center. There were no angels or people from my past. Previous events didn't flash before me. There was only the promise of release and relief. And also, there was this: a heightened consciousness of Me, of a Self existing separately from the body, and the sudden knowledge that living isn't necessarily a function of the body so much as it is an experience of the mind and the mind is energy and energy is indestructible and energy can take many forms and even separated from the body that energy exists.

As I moved deeper into the tunnel, I accepted this was the end. More than that, I sought its salvation and peace. I glided toward some other place that exuded tranquility; in which I felt strong and invincible; in which I felt awake and aware and filled with an incredible amount of my own energy and self-consciousness and power. I was hyperaware of my own unearthly existence. Not only that, I was completely at ease and in love with it. My self in the tunnel was incredibly large and vast and boundless. It was tremendous and I loved it. Apart from my body I became completely, surprisingly aware that at that very separate moment, I was more strong, more powerful, more omniscient and omnipresent than I had ever been or imagined I could be.

I loved this feeling. I embraced it and felt safe within it. I never wanted it to end. Instead, I wanted to feel this energy more and more. I wanted to expand within it, to live in this state of bliss and freedom. To end the nightmare and let a new dream begin. I wanted to go further into the tunnel and felt myself moving toward there.

And then I remembered my parents, who were working so hard on my behalf. I couldn't just leave them without a word. I paused in my move toward the darkness. I forced myself back down into my body and the light just far enough to call out to my parents and say,

I love you.
Thank you.
I'm dying.

If I'd taken time to think about their response, I would have assumed my parents would beg me to hang on. I would have expected them to cry and tell me I could make it, to try, for them. But I didn't think about what they would say. It didn't seem a possibility that I would live. I was already half gone, and there was nothing anyone could say that would make me give up the peace toward which I was moving, that would make me pledge allegiance again to a body in which I had felt so trapped and betrayed and in pain.

In the sudden silent stillness of the room, as the nurses froze, as my father stood stock-still, my mother didn't miss a beat. In a soft Southern drawl that surfaces only when she's very, very tired, she said, "Michele, nobody dying makes this amount of noise."

Her face didn't register fear or sadness. My mother spoke as if she were merely stating a fact. As if she'd just answered my impending doom with a discussion of what to have for dinner. I was announcing something tragic and she just rolled over it with another wave of logic.

I paused for a second to stare at her. She remained unperturbed, the epitome of the mother I have always recognized. I may have felt altered by pain, but she remained steadfast, able to joke, full of clarity.

The ridiculousness of what she said in light of what I was experiencing struck me as funny. Somewhere inside, a flutter began. A ludicrous wiggle of mirth traveled up from my stomach, through my swollen and sore throat, until it sprang from my mouth as a choked laugh. Once the passage had been opened, full-fledged laughter followed. Sure, it was delirious but it was life-affirming. It reconnected me with my body. It provided a bond to the world that gained strength with every second that I, and then my mother and father, and then the nurses, all broke up laughing.

We laughed too uncontrollably for too long. Sometime during the act of laughing my attachment to that transcendental place severed. I landed fully back in my body with a resounding psychological thud. The tunnel evaporated.

The spell was broken.

My mother leaned in close and said, "Now look here, you will not die. You will live through this."

"I can't."

"You can."

"It's too painful."

"You can do it."

"I don't have the strength."

"You do. You just have to find it. Right this minute, you go down further, further into yourself than you've ever been, and you find the strength to pull yourself through."

"I can't do it."

"Courage is a choice, Michele. Make it."

My mother's eyes were big and black and unrelenting. There was no way to disobey her.

I closed my eyes.

I sank into my body.

I went in search of my strength.

PART TWO:

CONFUSION

Change

Those first years after my illness I arranged my life in a way that made me feel a sense of security and safety. During my hospital stay, facts had come to light about the prescribing doctor's negligence. There had been, for example, an undisclosed note in my file about a possible allergy to sulfa that he should have seen. Mom, Dad, Bret, and I held a family meeting in which we discussed the option of suing for malpractice. Our discussion centered on the role we would have to play in the suit, and we all quickly agreed: we did not want to relive the past. My hospital stay was relegated to The Things About Which We Do Not Speak. If anyone brought up anything about it—including the suggestion that I explore my feelings—I flew into a fit of anger and demanded silence. By the time I entered high school, none of us ever spoke about that wretched month at all.

I did, of course, think about it. Every night, for example, I went to bed and lay awake, remembering the nights I had so painfully waited for sleep. I obsessed about how long it took to feel drowsy, feeling the anxiety build. During the day this anxiety increasingly expressed itself as an obsession with time: How long did it take to complete a task? Could I complete it faster? How much time elapsed between one activity and another? As the years progressed, I perfected being able to plan every day down to the second, racing against the clock to see which of us would win. I built up a large collection of watches so that at any moment I could chart the passage of time.

Still, I didn't tell anyone about my increasing anxiety and insomnia. Nor did I mention that sometimes, my mind just felt stuck. My gaze would land somewhere and lock while my mind drifted away, caught in some hospital memory, or nonspecific, shadowy feeling.

Instead of talking about these things I simply started turning the clocks away from me at night so I couldn't see them in the dark. I practiced not allowing memories to come too far into my head so I didn't have to feel what they brought with them. Even so, everything became a potential trap into which I might emotionally fall and the result would be an overwhelming blight of memory or feeling, or the eminent promise of a catastrophic event. Systematically I began controlling my emotions. I repressed joy. And happiness. Trust. Faith. Love. Instead of releasing feelings of grief, anger, and despair I denied any such feelings might exist. Regardless of how often my mother offered to talk (which she did many times), regardless of how often she suggested I might feel better if I did, I raged at the idea until she, too, fell silent. Rather than move through denial and depression and anger toward a new understanding of myself, I sank deeper into a definition *against* rather than *of* myself. I sank deeper into an internal silence, too, until finally, there was no voice at all.

When I reached Scarsdale High School I fell in with a crowd of girls my age and guys a few years older. I studied a lot, took advanced classes, managed the track team, worked on the yearbook, founded a literary magazine, and picked up horseback riding. I wrote letters to local hospitals offering myself as a contact for any SJS cases. When I didn't receive a single call, I volunteered at a hospital near our home. Every Saturday morning I dressed in my candy-striper uniform, carefully buttoning the top, smoothing the skirt, and feeling proud I was doing something meaningful. I worked the front desk or wheeled patients around the halls. I had an urge to help others not suffer the way I did. I decided I would eventually become a nurse.

Being busy made it easier to hide the fact that in many subtle ways, SJS had changed the shape of who I was. Running from one activity to another meant I didn't have much time to contemplate how my illness demanded I split off certain parts of myself, or how I had begun to see things from an altered point of view. Everything I had accepted before—the values of my family and society I had never questioned—became something to examine and reassess.

The spring I turned fifteen I was walking past a park near our home one day. It was a place I had played since I was two. I'd spent many happy hours in the sandbox, on the swings, and slipping down the slide. On this day, however, I looked at the children playing and the women sitting on benches and rocking strollers and a sudden, unfamiliar swell of revulsion swept over me. I stood still for a moment trying to understand what I felt. It wasn't revulsion for the children—but, yes, it was. It was revulsion for what they represented: the need for someone to set aside a part of herself for the benefit of someone else. The mere thought of having to divide myself again created a wave of enormous anxiety. "I don't ever want kids," I thought.

The realization that motherhood would not be an option for me felt absolutely natural, like the piece of a puzzle snapping into place. I took a deep breath and walked past the park feeling lighter, as if one of the parts of me was dusting off her hands saying, "Well, that's done."

Safety comes from knowing there are things you can count on. Boundaries, supports, undeniable facts. Make the world small and you know exactly your place in it and also, the dangers that threaten to get too close. My family was very dedicated to the idea of religion and the Jewish tradition. I had begun Hebrew School at the age of six. At the time of my illness I was fluent in Hebrew and had been Bat Mitzvah'd. It had never occurred to me to question the presence of God or religion or its place in my universe. Now it did. I struggled with understanding how God could exist if something so awful had happened to me. I wondered how I could have felt so alone in that moment in the tunnel if God was supposedly hanging around. For a few years I wrestled with the Divine issue alone, then just before one of the most holy days on the Jewish calendar, I dropped the bomb on my devout parents when I was sixteen.

"I'm not going to temple this year on Rosh Hashanah," I announced to my mother one afternoon. "And I'm quitting Hebrew school."

I knew my parents wouldn't like these decisions but participating in religious activities seemed hypocritical. And there was also this: the idea of God and religion overwhelmed me with an enormous, fingernails-digging-into-the-palms-of-my-hands, violent rage.

"I don't believe in God. I don't want to go to any more religious events," I continued. "I don't believe in any of it."

"God gave you the strength to survive," my mother explained. "He was with you in your moments of need."

"No, he didn't."

"Yes, he did."

"I did that. You told me to go inside myself, and I did. It wasn't God in there."

My mother gave me the book *When Bad Things Happen to Good People*. I was unswayed. My father got involved and the three of us hashed out the subject, ending in an argument: I wanted to leave the faith and was told I was too young to make such a decision. I respected that as my parents, they had the final say. I attended Jewish holidays and events as often as they required, each time feeling a physical fury pulse through me whenever I stepped over a synagogue threshold.

I made it through high school in an increasingly moody state. Days went by when I was sullen and uncommunicative. My mother followed me around, asking, "What's wrong?" and offering to talk. Instead of appreciating the loving nature of her gesture, I snarled, "You like to fix things, but you can't fix this!" I growled to be left alone because the truth was, I didn't really know what was wrong. I just knew I felt darkness in my mind, and it would take me a few days to push it back.

Meanwhile, I continued working hard to shut down my emotions. I gave myself little tests. Could I withstand the sadness of a movie and not cry? Could I watch a film with graphic scenes of a burn victim and remain unmoved? Yes, with an increasingly easy flip of some internal switch, I could go dead inside and not feel a thing.

Starving

When I struggled with high school biology I gave up the idea of becoming a nurse. For college, I chose a university with a rigorous English department and went back to my first love, writing. I was seven years old when I wrote my first short story, eight when I wrote my first novel. I picked up poetry in junior high school and fiction in high school. When I left for Washington University in St. Louis, Missouri, I went with the intention of becoming some kind of writer.

I approached college with the same dedication I'd shown in high school: I studied a lot. I had a growing sense that I never knew enough. I had trouble concentrating. I couldn't remember things that I read. I'd go over whole paragraphs three or four times and still not remember the points being made. I began writing copious outlines of text-books and class notes so that I didn't have to worry whether or not I could remember something. I relaxed only when I'd memorized the outlines until I could see them as pictures in my mind.

I didn't like the food at school, so my diet consisted of salads, ice cream, pizza, and trail mix. I never thought twice about this change in healthy habits. I ate the way I always had: when I was hungry. I had always had a quick metabolism, so I never worried about weight gain. I didn't consciously note when my clothes began fitting a little tightly. I made a core group of friends, went to ballgames and frat parties and outdoor concerts, and spent the rest of my time in the library.

In the middle of October, casually and for no real reason, I stepped on a scale. At my pre-college physical I'd weighed 116 pounds on my almost five foot eight frame. To my shock, the scale registered 124. When had this happened? *How* had this happened? Clearly, while I was not paying attention, my body had done something behind my back. A surge of anxiety coursed through me.

Over the next several weeks, I plunged into an apprehensive depression. I set up vigilant systems to monitor my body and its actions. I ate less and less. It didn't matter that I tossed all night with hunger pangs; they felt *good*. They reminded me I was in charge. With my body in crisis, suddenly I felt very alive.

Concentrating on how quickly I could take off the

weight became a full-time obsession. This was easy as all the girls I knew had started dieting, too. For them, it was about losing ten or fifteen pounds. For me, it wasn't about the number on the scale. It was about starving myself so that at the end of each day I'd know that I, not the body, had prevailed. By the time I went home for Christmas break six weeks later, I had lost twelve pounds. I felt strong and proud and fiercely protective of this new self I was developing. I wouldn't let anything interfere with her, not my mother's ashen face when she saw my gaunt body step off the plane, nor my father's pursed lips as he took hold of my scrawny arm and guided me to the car.

Christmas break became one long argument as I lied about what I ate, when I ate, and whether I had eaten at all. My parents were worried; I was scornful. I screamed and yelled and demanded to be left alone. Eventually I went back to school promising I would eat, knowing that was a flat-out lie. I got back to St. Louis, sank further into depression, and restricted food even more.

Throughout the spring semester as my despondency deepened and my anxiety enlarged, I became aware of a palpable disconnection between myself and my body. It and I were enemies locked in a vicious battle. It didn't help that I had come to hate WashU's campus, which was located in the midst of suburbia and incredibly cut off. On days I felt suffocated by the darkness in my mind I locked my dorm room door, turned up the stereo, and free-style danced until I was sweaty, relieved, and exhausted. Daily I called my mother in tears and then refused her offer to fly out and take a hotel room near campus. I was afraid that if I leaned on her for support, I would give up all my strength and then she, again, would be responsible for making me gain it back.

I tried to bring myself out of depression by making new friends. One of them introduced me to Evan, a frizzy-haired blond kid from Brooklyn. It wasn't until after we began dating that I discovered he was incredibly controlling and nasty. He'd scream at me, apologize, bring flowers, and then the cycle would begin again. Sometimes I argued back, but I didn't really have the energy to care and besides, I was so far inside my mind I was never fully present anyway.

Toward the end of the semester, Evan announced he loved me. "Come on, baby, let me be your first," became his constant refrain. While I had fooled around a little in high school, I had no real experience with sex. It was because I hated Evan that I eventually decided he would be the perfect person to lose my virginity to: no feelings, no ties to any entrapping emotional bond, no one to whom I felt bound to split off another piece of myself. I screwed Evan and dumped him at the beginning of summer vacation.

I spent the summer between my freshman and sophomore years at home working for a temp agency and fighting with my parents. My mother did all she could to get me to eat, and when that didn't work demanded I see an eating disorder therapist. Many arguments later, I gave in. At the end of the first session the therapist pronounced, "You have body image issues." I disagreed. She insisted. I drove around for an hour afterward to quell my rage. The truth was, I didn't care about my body, but I didn't know how to express or explain that. What I did instead was refuse to go back to therapy.

Held within the family cocoon that summer, I was able to somewhat commit to the structure of mealtimes. In the fall, when I transferred to the University of Pennsylvania, I went to campus armed with homemade blueberry muffins and an index card container of recipes.

I settled into UPenn and, again, studied all the time. It didn't take long for my self-destructive habits to return. I began starving myself, this time not just to take off unexpected weight or to beat my body into submission, but as a test: How long could I go without food and still study and function? I counted the hours until I got so hungry I could no longer put together a sentence, or I felt dizzy and faint. Only then would I allow myself a single slice of pizza. More and more I craved the feeling of starvation. The more separate I felt from my body, the more I liked feeling the pain it was in.

By the middle of the first semester I came down with an extreme case of flu, with a fever of 104. Instead of going to the doctor, I continued to study. I didn't want to miss my midterm exams. I was taking upper-level classes and couldn't afford to skip a session. I ignored my symptoms until I passed out in my dorm room and my roommates carried me to a cab and the emergency room.

I was ill and dehydrated. A nurse stuck me in a small space behind a curtain with a chair and a bed.

"I'll be right back with your IV."

Panic. "No!" The urge to cry, my body trembling.

"It's either that or you immediately drink a gallon of water." Fighting a growing nausea, I drank the water.

My parents arrived from Scarsdale at 2 a.m. They took me home, where I spent the next couple of weeks recuperating before returning to school.

This was a cycle that would repeat for the next twenty years: Push my body beyond its limit, collapse, go home, heal, pick up the pieces, then start it all over again.

Adaptation

By my junior year of college the pressure of confusion, depression, and anxiety had become overwhelming. I decided to let loose. Even though I didn't drink, I frequented all the bars on campus. I needed to be out. I was too afraid of my body to experiment with drinking or drugs, but I hung around places where people did, because those were the ones who were up all night, too. My insomnia had grown to such proportions that I slept only one to two hours a night; it was easier not to be home. I hid depression with an exuberance that fooled everyone. I dated one and then another and another of the football team. I worked as a DJ and then a cocktail waitress in a bar on campus. I ate little and detached from myself more and more.

I had enrolled in the Annenberg School of Communications so that I could get a dual degree in English and Communications. That meant staying at school over the summer, which was fine with me. My relationship with my parents had grown severely strained. We argued constantly about my weight, my health, and my resistance to seeking psychiatric help. Classes, and an internship at the local ABC affiliate, were the perfect excuse to stay in Philadelphia for the summer.

When the summer session began, my food regimen consisted of nothing except seltzer water until around three o'clock, then one green apple. Dinner was a bowl of rice. Finally, one night I was so overwhelmed by a ravenous, uncontrollable hunger that I found myself sitting on the kitchen floor ripping apart and devouring an entire roasted turkey. When I was finished, and the bones and skin lay scattered, I felt crazy, frightened of what was happening in my mind, and sick to my stomach. I called my mother.

"I need help," I told her bluntly.

My father arrived the next day, packed me up, and drove me home. My mother spent the summer researching therapists who specialized in eating disorders, and then convincing me to go. The results were always the same. I didn't want to talk. Beyond that, I simply didn't know what to say and was afraid of what would happen if I did. While I knew how I felt, I didn't know what I felt, or why or how to express it to someone else. I couldn't translate feelings into language and so, sitting in the office of therapist after therapist, I remained silent. I didn't see any of them more than once.

At home with my family, however, I found my footing. While my behaviors were still aberrant, they were less so and I attained some steady balance. My mother took me back to school for senior year and stayed with me in my apartment for a week. At the beginning of September, my hair fell out in a massive shedding. Mom and I looked at the strands in the tub and said, "It's because of the stress of the last six months."

That final year of college, I kept to myself in my apartment. I went to class and came right home. I studied and began writing plays to pass the time. I didn't socialize or hang out with friends or work in the bar. I felt safer and more stable being alone. While I didn't eat much, I ate more than before. I started counting calories and allowed myself no more than 1,200 a day. At that number I felt safe and still had total control. I got a gym membership and began working out or swimming at least one hour each day.

With no career plan, I graduated and moved to New York City. The feeling of the separated selves was now an accepted constant and although I recognized them, I still didn't know which one was supposed to be in charge. I felt an increasing distance from the present moment. More and more often I was aware that there was my body and then there was me, as if the real me existed outside of my body. I became expert at hiding these thoughts and the depressive melancholy that shadowed me. With people other than family, I faked smiles, happiness, and laughter. When alone, I walked around in a fog of depression.

I took whatever jobs were offered to me: advertising first, then publishing. I moved to the Upper West Side of Manhattan, where I shared a studio apartment with a girl I met on the train. Eventually, I fell into a job in entertainment public relations. Out every night of the week at events and with clients, in the office all day, no time to think, feel, or sit still, I found entertainment PR the perfect way to reimplement my old coping mechanisms. Once again I began running from one thing to another. I felt relieved, functional, and normal.

A year and a half passed before the constant parties, no sleep, no food, and the stress of staving off an enormous melancholy and depression caught up with me. I collapsed and was diagnosed with Epstein-Barr Virus (EBV). Which turned into Chronic Fatigue Syndrome (CFS). Which brought with it an acute case of fibromyalgia. I could barely get out of bed. I went home to Scarsdale to recuperate.

When I was well enough to return to the city, my parents helped support me while I launched a little PR business from my apartment. With a few freelance clients, I attempted to regain my strength while working at my own pace. I was dating Mark, a former client and the owner of a nightclub downtown. His family had a house by the Jersey shore, and on weekends he took me there to rest and relax. With the free time of convalescence, I turned my attention to writing again. I took a playwriting class in which I met a director who wanted to produce and direct one of my plays Off-Off Broadway. I should have been excited about this but instead it felt unimportant, as if it was a thing that was happening for someone else.

Writing, however, was good for me. It gave me a focus outside my physical discomfort and limitation. It gave me something in which to bury the emotional angst I carried and also a place to explore how and when and why to find language and choose words. I began by writing plays I thought were about serious characters who felt lost or trapped. In rehearsal for that first play, however, we discovered I had actually written a comedy. Afterward, I stuck to being funny and turned out plays guaranteed to produce laughs. My brother, Bret, graduated college and moved to Manhattan. We shared an apartment and he became my script editor. Evenings we sat at the kitchen table reading through the copy I'd written during the day, refining it, adding another layer of humor as our collaboration opened up new ideas.

It took two years to fully recuperate from EBV/CFS. Around the end of this time, Mark started talking about marriage. The few friends I had were getting engaged and, in the middle of my twenties, I thought I should consider doing the same. I tried to feel love for Mark. I pretended I did love him. But what I really felt was a stomachache. Whether or not Mark was 'the one', the whole notion of marriage made me feel trapped, in danger of losing another part of myself. I came to understand that I would never be someone's wife. When Mark and I split I felt tremendous relief.

Finally I felt well enough to return to full-time work. I signed up with a temp agency. The plan was to temp three weeks of the month—enough to cover rent, food, and utilities—and spend the rest of the time writing. A few months into the plan, I took an assignment at a money management firm. After a few days my boss offered me a permanent position. The pay, the hours, and the simplicity of the work were too good to refuse. I rejoined the workforce feeling my life, finally, was on a genuine track. I was healthy, working, and going to be a writer after all.

The stability of this new job suited me. I worked with a great group of people who laughed all day. I socialized with them outside of work. I joined the company softball team. I started dating Jared, a computer tech whose office was across from mine. I wrote every night after work, or attended rehearsal for one of my plays. Jared introduced me to mountain biking, and on the weekends we took long rides in the backwoods of New Jersey or Delaware or Vermont, where the company had a ski lodge. Jared knew how to make me laugh. Around him I dropped the strictness of my systems. We ate, even overate. My body bloomed and curved as my weight climbed to 130 pounds. I felt good and solid. For the first time I felt happy and as if, finally, the right self might be assuming control. I wasn't fine, but I was much less wound up, anxious, and jittery. And now, every time my mind slipped away there was Jared, holding my hand, saying, "Welcome back," when I once again pulled myself into the present.

Behold the Zebra! (Again)

I was twenty-nine when a trigger sent me into a tailspin. I had come down with yet another sinus infection. For a couple of years I'd been getting them every three months, shutting me down with intense pain and, after my steely resistence, ultimately necessitating a trip to the doctor and a prescription for antibiotics. In the winter of 1997 my doctor was away. When the symptoms finally became too much to bear, I made an appointment with a new internist.

From the moment I entered his office, I didn't feel comfortable with this doctor. He was condescending and didn't seem to listen to me. He wouldn't look me in the eye. When he suggested I take an antibiotic with which I was unfamiliar, I reminded him, "I have a history. . . . My body is sensitive."

"You'll be fine," he said, scribbling on a pad. "We routinely use Biaxin to cure sinus infections."

"Are you sure—"

"You'll be all right!"

I so badly wanted to trust the doctor. I so badly wanted to stop fighting against my brain's shutting down, or the feeling of panic. I was in pain and not thinking straight. I chastised myself for resisting, then filled the prescription and took the medication.

Within forty-eight hours I had a violent reaction. For a week my gastrointestinal system rebelled in every possible way. Finally, the doctor switched me to a new medication and we expected my body to adjust. It did not.

Suddenly I could barely eat. I could keep down only baked potatoes and rice. My newly gained weight dropped quickly. For two months I ate less and less while my body launched an all-out revolt. And then one day, it just shut down. After a walk in Central Park with my father, I fainted. He put me in the car and took me home to Scarsdale where, over the next few months, my physical state deteriorated rapidly. I could barely eat even one cracker. I lost twenty pounds, plus my ability to care for myself.

My parents and I made the rounds to various doctors. Lab reports showed that my small intestine wasn't working the way it should, which made my stomach not work the way it should, which made other organs—liver, pancreas—not work the way they should. Still, no doctor could pinpoint the problem. I bounced from specialist to specialist searching for a cure, only to be told that my condition defied medical knowledge. No one could prescribe relief for the host of food allergies I developed, the nausea, the cramping, the bloating, the sudden lactose intolerance, the incredible permeability of my gut that allowed no absorption of nutrients. After a few months I managed to eat small amounts of unseasoned chicken and steamed vegetables, but my body would not hold on to it.

For a while I took seventeen vitamins, supplements, and prescription medications designed to nourish me and digest food for me. Still, my calcium and magnesium levels were dangerously low. My liver enzymes rose worrisomely high. Vitamin B counts barely made it onto the charts. I hovered at the borderline of anemia. My muscles and joints burned and ached. At the beginning of September my hair, which, since my senior year of college, thinned each autumn and then struggled to grow in the rest of the year, again fell out at an alarming rate. My abdomen was so puffed out that strangers congratulated me on my pregnancy. Test after test returned and there were two kinds of bad news. The first, some concrete problem. The second, no diagnosis at all, which meant nothing to cure. As a result of all of this I became increasingly isolated. I ended things with Jared and kept up with friends only through short, infrequent phone calls. I kept to myself as depression and doctor visits filled each day.

Eventually, I stabilized enough to return to the city, where I continued to subject myself to specialists and more tests. Walking down hospital corridors, being hooked up to machines, having blood drawn, being referred to another specialist for another battery of tests I didn't feel afraid. I didn't feel a thing. Even when I went all the way up to Yale's Center for Digestive Diseases I walked like an automaton, resigned and stoic and detached. I sat in the waiting rooms of gastroenterologists, liver specialists, endocrinologists, internists, parasitologists, and allergists. I submitted to their pokes, prods, and needles and waited for them to cure me. When Western medicine offered no answers, I turned to alternative outlets. Mondays I took the subway to see Dr. Ng in Chinatown, who sent me home with packets of herbs and pills and a disgusting concoction of roots and fungi to brew into a nasty-tasting tea. On Tuesdays a nutritionist met with me in my home. On Wednesdays I visited a homeopath in Chelsea for an IV vitamin drip. Thursdays I had a standing appointment for reflexology on Park Avenue South. Fridays I saw a New Age chiropractor downtown. His favorite process: manipulating my back to "release negative emotions." Although the physical pain he caused reduced me to tears, he assured me this was the path to wellness. In desperation I even tried to work over the phone with a healer in Hawaii.

My life became my illness; management of my un-named illness became my life. I dragged around a bony, exhausted, and pain-filled body when I had the strength to drag around at all. I lost my job. I spent months in bed, using up my savings to pay rent. My body sank into chaos, and my psyche perched on the brink of destruction. I was ultimately diagnosed with mercury poisoning and Celiac Disease but despite treatment, nothing changed. My days were full of undefined illnesses that led to defined illnesses that led to more mysteries. No matter what I did, my primary identity remained a patient.

Sixteen years after SJS, I was a medical anomaly, alone, a freak, a zebra all over again.

Month after month my mother accompanied me to every medical appointment and test as doctor after doctor tried to figure out what, exactly, had gone wrong. Together Mom and I sat in waiting rooms—she dressed and made up, thinking positively, reading a magazine, and looking ready for business; me (now thirty pounds lighter) in jeans two sizes too big and old stretched-out T-shirts, glumly staring into space. Again my mother tried to talk to me about my thoughts and feelings and suggested I seek psychiatric guidance. I responded, "There's nothing wrong with my head; it's my stomach that's the problem."

"It might be helpful for you to tell someone how you're feeling about all of this."

"I don't want to talk about what's wrong. I want someone to fix it. I want someone to cure me, not chat with me."

"This is all so emotionally draining for you."

"I can handle it! I'm not crazy!!"

This idea I wasn't crazy, though, was one I was privately struggling to secure. Recently in my starved state, I had begun hallucinating the odors of food. As if that wasn't enough, I had begun to spontaneously cry—everywhere. In doctors' offices and retail stores, I released great public heaving breaths of anguished weeping. There I'd be, walking in Riverside Park, when a sudden whoosh of emotion would knock me into a state of teary hysteria. In these moments I centered myself by finding a way to prove I was not crazy. I stood still. I let the emotion swell and waited for it to subside. I controlled my breathing and observed my surroundings with great concentration until I could smell the polluted New York City air and look dry-eyed at a stranger walking past.

A year and a half into the Magical Mystery Tour of Undefined Chronic Illness, in December 1998, the levees finally gave way. I pinned my hopes on a world-famous celebrity doctor in Manhattan and spent a day in his office having blood drawn and tests administered, and submitting to several physical and psychological assessments and interviews. Finally, I met with the Guru himself.

He was seated at his desk looking through some pages in a folder. I sank into a dark-green leather, brass-studded chair and waited for him to prescribe a miracle cure. He was a big man, tall and wide and looking all the more so because his desk was huge and he did not seem small in comparison. He was reading my lab reports, pieces of yellow, green, and pink pages that he studiously shuffled. At last, he huffed and shook his head and drew up his eyes to look at me. We regarded each other for a moment, and then he shrugged his enormous shoulders and scattered the pages.

Hands clasped on top of his large, paper-filled desk, he looked at me in silence.

Finally, he shrugged again, shook his head, and said, "I don't know what this is."

I stared at him in disbelief.

"I haven't seen a case this complicated in . . . " He looked at the ceiling and calculated his own history. "Seven years."

"But you think you can help."

Pursing his lips and shuffling my reports, he said, "No, I'm afraid I can't."

He finished arranging my file without another word. As the quiet continued, it dawned on me the meeting was over. I began to feel a sort of crazy, childish panic. I slid to the edge of my seat and leaned toward the doctor.

"That can't be all there is. I've spent the whole day here. I've had all these new tests. I've talked to your entire staff. There have to be answers."

The Guru's brow knit.

"I'm afraid I'm stumped."

I stared at him in silence.

"I'm sorry," he said, standing up.

I didn't stand up. I couldn't. I was stunned. I was used to doctors not having answers. I was even getting used to them having answers that were wrong. But I was completely unprepared for one who would not even try to suggest something that might bring me relief.

The Guru moved toward the door, opened it, and stood waiting for me to walk through.

I stepped out of the office into the December cold and walked west.

The city was already mounting its huge display of holiday cheer. The electric snowflake sparkled above Fifth Avenue. Saks's windows hosted those signature motorized scenes I'd loved as a little girl. That evening, however, it all annoyed me. There were too many people jostling me in the street. The air was too cold, the wind too searing. There were too many sparkling holiday promotions and the city bustled with an enormously irritating influx of happy tourists.

I shivered beneath five layers of sweaters, two scarves, thick gloves, and a hat. Irrational and unstoppable tears spilled onto my cheeks. As I walked hunched and Grinch-like in the early dusk, I imagined myself wasting away to a skeleton. A single thought plagued me: If the top doctors in New York City could not help me, what would become of me? How would I survive? How could I survive if no one could figure out what was wrong or how to cure me? How could I exist if I kept losing weight? I saw nothing in the future except my slow, starved deterioration. There was my body, with its skin hanging loosely over its skeleton; and me, wandering the streets searching for a cure. I had already survived being the zebra once. I didn't feel I'd be so lucky again.

As I turned south onto Park Avenue, the tears poured out. Too tired for embarrassment, I stood there watching the after-work crowd shuffle by with heads down into the wind. Motionlessly, I let the tears quietly flow. Then I sobbed until I was completely worn out.

Finally, I went to the nearest pay phone. My father's office sat a few blocks away. When my father answered the phone, I burst into a fresh round of tears.

"Michele? What's wrong? Where are you?"

I couldn't answer. My mother was the office manager. In a second her voice was on the line.

"Michele, what's happened?"

"He can't help me," I said between sobs.

"Oh, honey. . . ."

"What's going to happen to me? What am I going to do?"

"Maybe it's time for you to get a different kind of help."

The Cocoon

When I scheduled my initial appointment with Greg, the idea was that he would help me develop coping skills for living with mysterious illness. I agreed to meet him for one reason: Greg's practice was founded on principles of both psychotherapy and spirituality. I had no interest in therapy, but a man who understood and focused on spirituality seemed like a man to whom I could relate. Since I graduated college I had put my foot down and stopped going to synagogue. In place of religion I had developed a personal transcendental focus that depended on my own self rather than some unproven entity. A therapist who believed in spirituality would, I thought, at least not infringe on those efforts.

I walked from my apartment to Greg's office on an extremely cold day. Instead of taking the elevator (which would have been easier in my frail condition), I took the stairs to the second floor. You don't stay tough, ready for the next challenge, by taking the easy route anywhere. Weak and out of breath after only four steps up the first flight, I sat down to rest. My fibromyalgic muscles screamed and burned. After several pauses I finally reached Greg's office exhausted and faint.

"Hello," he said with a smile, and stood aside to let me pass through the door.

Immediately his presence hooked me. He was tall, six feet four, and trim, with short, black-speckled gray hair neatly parted on the left side. His eyes, a pewter color, were warm and friendly with a sparkle hinting at his quick sense of humor. Greg's deep, smooth voice was incredibly mellow and seemed to flow effortlessly from his mouth, as if he was merely exhaling a breath and there happened to be words floating on it.

He moved with easy grace. He had an aura of such comfort in his own skin that I immediately felt centered and grounded and safe just standing beside him. I curled up in a stuffed blue upholstered chair, tucking my legs beneath me. Greg shut the door to the office, and the dimly lit room turned inward upon itself like a cocoon.

The first few weeks Greg and I focused on the events of the previous year and a half: my sudden illness and the inability of any doctor to diagnose or cure it.

"Tell me how this all got started," Greg suggested. And so I launched into an historical account. At the end of my story, Greg said, "Tell me your overall feeling in relation to what you've been dealing with for the past year and a half."

I had been looking at the African photographs on Greg's wall, but then I leveled my gaze on him.

"Powerlessness. I feel completely, utterly powerless."

"Anything else?"

"I should have been more careful. If I had just done some research about Biaxin . . . I wasn't paying attention. I was irresponsible. I was caught with my guard down."

"And your guard is always up?"

"Yes. I never know when my body might surprise me. That day, though, I was tired of being hyper-careful all the time. I wanted to be happy and carefree, not always living with this shadow of trepidation and distrust. I wanted to give over the sense of always having to be in control in order to feel safe. And I wanted to stop dragging around the past, as if every time I walk into a medical situation I might end up with a mysterious illness no one's ever seen, and another one of those moments when I feel I'm dying."

I was silent for a moment, reflecting on and trying to understand my own actions. Greg waited for me to continue. "I guess, Greg, I was sick of my own history and my enslavement to it, so I just shut up and did what the doctor ordered."

"You'd never done that before?"

I shook my head. "I'm always resisting medical advice. I'd rather suffer what I know is happening than risk what I don't know might happen. For a long time after SJS I wouldn't even take a Tylenol. But this time I was so sick, and in so much discomfort, and I was so tired; so sick and tired of always feeling like I had to be running in front of something bad. I wanted to feel normal for a change. I wanted not to be the patient who's always anxious and driving people crazy. I wanted to feel like I was safe. It was stupid. It was the only time I've done that, and I paid for it."

A brief pause. Greg waited for me to speak again. When I didn't, he said, "Are there other times in your life you've felt powerless?"

"Yes."

"When?"

A brief pause. "September 1981."

TALKING WITH GREG was like being released from the circus. I no longer had to perform. I no longer had to convince myself or anyone else I was all right, stable, happy, or any of the other things that, when you're ill and disgusted by pity, you try to fake. I could admit I was afraid, without hope that I would ever feel at peace. I felt secure in the knowledge that if I started to fall apart, Greg would catch me.

Under Greg's tutelage and through a forced devotion to a sort of cognitive consciousness, I began to reconnect with myself in both physical and psychological realms. Over a period of six months the pain in my muscles somewhat diminished. I could walk without feeling I was using an insufficient amount of weak and weary ligaments to haul a heavy skeleton up the block. With Greg, I admitted how old fears were hanging around and messing with my head. I saw how my fear of medicine made me act irrationally: either I was overly cautious about prescriptions, combing over definitions in the *Physicians' Desk Reference* and grilling pharmacists, or I threw back pills without a second thought. Through speaking with Greg I recognized how my survival techniques had gotten a little out of hand.

Together, we forged an understanding and knowledge of the core issues so that I developed the ability to alter myself. We clarified topics grounded in the past and defined their repercussions in the present. I learned to redesign my reactions to new events by understanding the motivating principles of my responses. We brought light into the darkness of my fear, and we did it without overwhelming me, so that not only did I begin to function better outside Greg's office but I became increasingly in control and adept within it.

All this seemed to happen without my really being aware of it. Greg was a sort of magician, and changes occurred in me as a consequence of the knowledge he showed me how to pull out of my very own hat.

Which is not to say I didn't fight Greg and the whole process from day one.

"I don't want to go back there!" I'd say whenever he probed the memories of my first illness. "Talking makes me sad and melancholy. I don't want to go so far into it I can't come out. I don't want to spend the days between our visits in a fog of depression and despair. Although," and here I was struck by that unwitting second of clarity good therapy brings about, "that's not really so different from how I already spend each day."

With this realization my attitude began to change. I started to go back closer to 1981 than Greg's questions even suggested. Once I got going, I gave more detail than Greg may have wished, but I couldn't stop myself. For so many years these memories had been kept behind a curtain in my mind that when I was finally brave enough to pull the curtain aside, it was a relief.

Precisely because Greg and I were unknown to each other, our work together gained strength. I had nothing invested in his reactions to me. I had nothing to lose by baring all to him, showing him that beneath my veneer of stoic strength I was cowering, and beyond that: I found a sort of solace in knowing it.

"When I'm happy and not worrying, things get out of control. It's not okay for me to be okay. When things seem all right I don't take good care," I admitted one afternoon. "I feel most safe when I don't feel safe. As if feeling fear keeps me alert and will ultimately keep me from harm. I can't explain it, but not feeling safe reminds me to be aware and to remember who I am. I'm a survivor and if I don't remember what happened, it could happen again. Fear feels familiar."

"That's completely normal, but by holding on to that feeling of powerlessness, how do you ever expect to be free of it?"

"I don't want to be free of it. It reminds me who I am. Sometimes I feel so lost. I can't see myself at all, except as a person who survived this horrific thing. In the context of that tragedy is the only time I know exactly who I am. The past is what feels most real. The rest is only a fantasy."

"You can choose your own reality, Michele."

"I choose the truth."

"The truth is, you were strong enough to survive. There's nothing powerless about that."

Inner Wisdom

About a month after our first meeting, Greg taught me transcendental meditation. I lay on the maroon couch in his office and closed my eyes while he talked me through the process of relaxing my body and identifying a word upon which to focus. The word I chose was *peace,* and with my eyes closed, listening to Greg's soft voice, I shrugged off the world and tried to manufacture a state of being I had never consciously known.

Greg's purpose in teaching me to meditate reached beyond helping me develop some sort of mind control. He believed meditation would encourage a reconnection with my body. Developing dialogue and trust between my body and my self would, he suspected, act as a source of both physical and emotional healing. In these early days our conversations were geared toward my finding a way to quell the anxiety related to my health. We spoke at length about my original illness and what I experienced and how I adapted afterward. Our discussions broadened from there to include a focus on reconnecting with my healthy, safe, individual self which, we discovered, I could not imagine. When the bond between my self and my body broke, when my trust of the outer world disintegrated, my consciousness and sense of instinct and intuition suffered. Afterward the deafening din of terror silenced my internal voice. With Greg, I worked to retrieve all of what I once possessed.

I began looking forward to our sessions. Alone, I compartmentalized thoughts and fears and lived with the sound of them rattling in their boxes. With Greg, however, I removed the lids and was surprised to find that what I always expected—those unrestrained emotions would lead to my complete dissolution—did not occur. Putting things into words did not release me from their effects but did take some of the mystery out of whether or not I could tolerate integrating those thoughts and feelings into my present self. I found that I could. I learned to voice the thoughts I usually suppressed about my physical situation and about the memories I strove to deny. I spoke openly about certain small fears and groped for words to express the larger ones. Finally, I was able to admit and describe the emotions those fears aroused in me.

"Do you think," I mused one day toward the end of a session, "if I had tried talking about this stuff when I was thirteen, I could have done it?" I had just concluded a long and halting explanation of how I'd felt upon leaving the hospital. Saying the words hadn't been as difficult as I'd anticipated. "Do you think, maybe, I didn't need to wait eighteen years to get it all out?"

"Did you try?"

"No. I had a deep sense that speaking any of this would destroy me, like I was holding myself together by deliberately not talking about it. Also, I didn't have the words. When I thought about how to convey what I was thinking and feeling, all that came to mind was a very long scream."

"Maybe you needed time for the right words to form."

I thought about this for a minute and slowly nodded.

"Maybe you're right. Maybe I did."

"You trusted your inner wisdom."

"Or I trusted fear."

"The Ego voice, which is fear, usually suggests we do the opposite of what we need. It worries that if we are well and carefree, it will have no purpose."

"So, then, the sense that talking wasn't right was . . . wrong."

"Only if it was the Ego voice you were following. If your inner voice was directing you, then it would be right."

"How can you tell the difference between the two voices?"

"One you hear; the other you feel."

"So, then, the sense that talking wasn't right was . . . right."

"Perhaps."

I had never considered that I might have made good decisions in the aftermath of SJS. I did what I needed to do in order to survive; nothing had been consciously thought out. Looking at the situation from this perspective, though, I recognized I had done what was right for me: I'd proceeded on feeling.

I looked at Greg with a strange sense of enlightenment.

"In all that chaos, I had good instincts."

"You did. You still do."

"I wasn't as lost as I felt."

Greg smiled and shook his head. "Perhaps not."

We sat in silence while I thought about what this implied. And then it occurred to me: The power we discover inside ourselves as we survive a life-threatening experience can be utilized equally well outside of crisis, too. I am, in every moment, capable of mustering the strength to survive again—or of tapping that strength in other good, productive, healthy ways.

Poetry

I quit writing for theater the year I began working with Greg. Suddenly, comedy was boring. I tried writing a serious play; I couldn't do it. The script was stagnant and overburdened by my need and complete inability to communicate what I really wanted to say. I switched to writing poetry, which seemed to be a shorter, more manageable form. I believed it would force me to write from a deeper place while ensuring I didn't get so lost inside my head I'd never find my way back out. I found Martha, a New York University teacher, to tutor me and paid for the sessions with money I made at my new job in children's publishing, another temp position that had yielded a formal offer.

Every Thursday I stuffed a sheaf of papers into my bag and took the subway to Martha's apartment in Greenwich Village where, over the course of an hour, she taught me to transform the thoughts I had into crafted lyric poems composed of lines, stanzas, and metaphors. It was slow going at first. Writing comedy had allowed me to remain at a distance from what I thought and felt. Writing a poem, however, forced me to get close to those things I shied away from. Finally, I began writing around, if not about, the thoughts I tried to suppress. I built a small portfolio of poems and Martha suggested I begin submitting my work for publication.

"And you should get out to some poetry readings," she said. "You need to listen to how poetry sounds out loud. Different kinds of poetry, too. Not just traditional, but poetry slams as well."

Three weeks later I worked up the nerve to attend a

"slam," a poetry competition where poets read or recite work and are judged on a numeric scale. The poems are often vitriolic and sound like the step-sibling of rap. Pete was sitting on a bar stool, and when I walked by we recognized each other. He had been the manager of a club owned by one of my publicity clients. He was handsome with enormous, feeling brown eyes, a quick smile, and muscular build. He had left the club business and was now directing commercials.

"But what I really want to do is produce a slam poetry show," he explained between sips of beer.

Pete initiated me into the slam scene and encouraged me to write slam poetry and perform it. He was ambitious, creative, passionate, strong, charismatic, and full of a self-confidence I had never possessed. He was also smart, challenging, completely present, and over-flowing with energy. Around him some instinctual, resilient self woke up in me.

Although he was married, Pete and I spent a lot of time together, meeting up for poetry readings and slam events. It seemed perfectly natural, when his marriage busted up a month later, that we begin dating. There were, of course, many good reasons not to do this, but Pete was so alive. Everything about him pulsed with an electrifying passion I couldn't resist. In my previous relationships, I had to man-ufacture emotions. With Pete, I immediately felt so much. As if I were waking from a coma, suddenly the whole world quivered. Pete challenged, aroused, and stimulated me. Being around him was exciting and frightening. Three weeks into our affair, one morning after Pete had spent the night he was leaving to meet his soon-to-be ex-wife. Knowing there was the possibility they could reconcile, I softly said, "I love you," as he walked out of my bedroom. I was thirty-one years old. I'd never said that to a man and actually meant it. Pete was furious.

"How can you tell me such a thing today?!"

I didn't care that the timing was wrong. I loved that, because of him, I felt myself changing. I loved that his presence made me feel free, safe, strong, and vulnerable all at the same time. I loved that I felt connected to someone. I wanted him to know it. Pete left, shaking his head, without answering.

Pete and his wife didn't reconcile. That night he and I went to dinner and he admitted he loved me, too. A few weeks later when he needed a place to stay, Pete moved in with Bret and me, which is when he began to discover my daily idiosyncracies. Finally, one morning he sat up in bed and said, "Are you really going to live the rest of your life this way? You're always so terrified of what you can and can't eat. You have to control everything. You always have to be right. You time each moment down to the last second. You never sleep through the night. No one unplugs every clock in the room before they go to bed! What's wrong with you?"

Pete was the first person to put this all to me so bluntly. I was quiet for a moment and then hesitantly, I told him my SJS secret. Pete's face softened and his body relaxed. He enfolded me in his arms.

"You have to work this all out."

It was a comfort to be with Pete while my therapy progressed. The longer we were together, however, the more I learned his secrets, too, namely, that he had major anger issues, drank too much, and smoked a lot of dope. Many times he screamed and yelled and cursed at me so much, I thought Bret would haul off and punch him. Twice I tried to break things off, but Pete would convince me how much he loved me and how he would be different and I, not wanting to give up what had brought feeling into my life, stayed with him.

Despite the hardships with Pete, I was feeling better. My work with Greg continued to evolve. Because of Pete's urging, I began experimenting with foods I hadn't eaten in a long time. I wasn't always successful. But Pete gradually wooed me back to taking chances, and sometimes things went all right and I would be surprised that my body was willing to re-engage in the pleasure of food. My writing took on more and more of a flow, too. I published my first poem, and then a book about rock bands written for the publisher for whom I worked. I became more of a full self: I defined boundaries, learned how to communicate, and started more consciously mulling the question, "What do I want?"

In the end, I did not want Pete. After almost a year together I kicked him out after one too many evenings full of lies, beer, and pot.

Shortly after that night I made a list of twenty-two things I was afraid of. At the top of the list: "I am afraid of myself." And yet, I wanted more and more to become myself. Writing seemed to be the path to that connection. I had been thinking about going back to graduate school for a Masters of Fine Arts in Poetry (MFA). Pete had ridiculed the idea. Without him around, it didn't seem so ridiculous at all.

Finding My Voice

O ver the next year my body gained strength. My insomnia became . . . manageable. My mind was avidly pushing itself forward. As Martha and I continued our weekly work, my portfolio of poems grew. I still could not directly write about my experiences or feelings or fears, but each poem got a little bolder or addressed a different part of my struggle. My own authentic voice had been silenced in 1981. Poetry was enticing it back and I was feeling empowered by it. Meanwhile, Greg and I continued our weekly conversations. With his guidance I began taking more control of my life. I quit my job in publishing and accepted a position teaching public relations at the Fashion Institute of Technology (FIT).

A little over a year after my split with Pete I entered the MFA program at Vermont College. I was afraid of committing to school full-time, so I chose a low-residency program: I would be on campus two weeks every semester and accomplish the rest of my coursework at home at my own pace.

The first semester went well. Martha and I stopped working together and I corresponded with the professor I was assigned at school. I wrote lyric, free verse poetry through the personas of various characters. Still, I shied away from the topics I needed to face. Each poem stuttered on the surface of thought. My voice splintered into many voices, and I went back to writing the way I had for theater: light, funny, going for laughs instead of substance.

In the second semester, everything changed. I was feeling good and doing well and decided I was done with therapy. I quit talking to Greg.

I was given a grant to spend a month at an artists' retreat in the summer of 2002. In the idyllic setting of a one-traffic-light town, I read and wrote and spent time with poets, novelists, painters, and sculptors. And I discovered the sonnet. A form of poetry dating back to the sixteenth century, sonnets are composed of fourteen lines metered out in strict rhyming structure. In the controlled context of the form I felt secure enough to approach the topics that most frightened me. Through a heavy reliance on metaphor, I began writing about my illness and my shattered identity afterward.

Almost immediately, my world began to unravel.

Insomnia was the first thing to intensify. I would be awake for twenty-four hours straight. I wrote all night. When FIT reopened, I wrote all night and then wrote and taught during the day. Eventually I'd crash and sleep for a few hours before bouncing awake and starting all over again. Finally, I broke down and begged my general practitioner for sleeping pills. I was too afraid to take them, and then too desperate not to. When I summoned the nerve, the pills allowed me to sleep for three to four hours.

In the fall my hair fell out in a sudden rush again more than ever before. I cut it all off so that I had a short bob and hid the scalp that showed through by wearing fat headbands, which gave me migraines, or putting my hair up in tiny clips that dug into the skin. My digestion imploded. I reverted to old food restrictions and managed my gastrointestinal symptoms by frequent starvation.

I continued to study and teach but otherwise minimized my contact with the outside world. Exhausted and in physical and emotional pain, I lay on my couch most of the day, pen and paper in hand, writing. By my third semester, I fell into a depression that took me deeper into despair than I had ever been. Sonnets flowed out of me in an endless stream. I developed an alter ego, a man, and began writing about his pain and loss and fears. With each poem I moved closer to acknowledging my own experience, but I could not use the word "I." The more sonnets I wrote, the more my body sank into a depleted state and my mind, already on overload, whirled itself into a hyperexhausted mess.

It wasn't exactly an opportune time for a puppy.

Nonetheless, the desire for one (which had been lurking around for a decade) welled up in me. I wanted—no, *needed* —a Soft-Coated Wheaten Terrier. The first time I'd ever seen this type of dog I'd been on East Fifty-fourth Street and dropped to my knees. Its eyes were soulful and human, its wriggly body so full of a pent-up joy that I had the urge to clasp the dog to my chest and never let go. Now, as my emotions overwhelmed me, I started accosting every Wheatie owner I saw, learning about the breed and gathering names of breeders. In May there was a litter in Sag Harbor, on eastern Long Island. "It's not the right timing," I told my mother. "I can't take on a puppy and teach and finish school."

"In life, Michele, it's never the right time. Get the puppy. You'll find a way to make it work."

Two weeks later my parents and I made the long drive to Sag Harbor. I sat on the floor of a woman's house as she brought out the puppies one at a time. The first and second were females and they leaped around, running after toys, nipping at my hair, and struggling to be free when I held them. Then, from across the room, she set a male puppy on the floor. His tiny brown and black body raced toward me. He ducked under my arm, climbed into my lap and sat down, curling his little form against me.

"This one's mine!" I announced.

I called him Baylee, a name that seemed both whimsical and human. With a sense of humor and a seemingly endless capacity for joy, Baylee made me laugh many times every day. I'd be on the couch mining my pain in poetry and Baylee would suddenly run through the apartment, head held high, his mouth trailing an enormous stream of toilet paper, still attached to the roll in the bathroom. I graded papers with one hand while throwing a ball with the other as he skidded and chased it across the floor.

Baylee had spunk, but he could also be incredibly peaceful. When I developed a bad head cold, he curled up on my chest and slept while I rested on the couch. His joyful presence touched something buried in me. Baylee's inquisitive eyes, his endlessly wagging tail, plus his habit of pawing at me to be picked up anchored me to every moment in a way that was fun and funny and full of pleasure.

As the summer went on Baylee grew, my writing progressed, and my head cold hung around until I always had an enormous headache and my eyes were puffy and swollen with pressure. I knew I probably had a sinus infection but I didn't want to go to the doctor or take another antibiotic. When the pain became unmanageable I broke down and went to see my otolaryngologist. He immediately sent me for a CAT scan. Sitting on a cold metal chair in his office, I listened to the diagnosis.

"You have a sinus infection that has reached the brain barrier. You need emergency surgery." I listened impassively to the news. Easily, I resigned myself, once again, to the role of patient.

I went into the operation with the detached fear that someone would make a mistake. To anyone near me I repeated over and over, "I'm allergic to sulfa."

The operation went well and I was sent home to Scarsdale to recuperate. The doctor knew of my adverse reactions to Codeine, so he prescribed a Tylenol-based painkiller. I popped the pills and went to sleep. I awoke a few hours later with an overwhelming nausea that sent me running into the bathroom. With my face bandaged and my head exploding in pain, I spent the next twenty-four hours hanging my head over the toilet. At first, we thought it was just the anesthesia wearing off. I took more painkillers and tried to rest. When I got worse instead of better, we phoned the doctor. It didn't take long to discover the mistake: Someone had reversed the instructions and given me straight Codeine.

I stayed in Scarsdale until FIT opened for the fall semester. My hair fell out again, the familiar ache and burn of fibromyalgia returned. Still, I plowed ahead with classes and my own studies. My poetry thesis developed into a manuscript of sonnets, and in my fourth semester, finally, I began using the word "I." At last, I stood in the center of my own experience. The darkness in my head became impenetrable. The fog in which I lived thickened. Once again I began bursting into tears in inexplicable moments. I existed more and more outside of every instant, seeing my body as a thing that walked through the city while I traveled outside of it.

When, the following January, I graduated with my MFA, I continued teaching at FIT but otherwise laid on the couch, exhausted, sleep-deprived, and in growing emotional and physical pain. I receded more from the world, even from my family. My mother reached out to help me; I only argued. My father tried to talk with me rationally; I pushed back and emotionally shut off. Bret sat me down to express how worried they all were about me. Nothing he said got through my anger and tears.

I began making the rounds of doctors again. My liver enzymes were skyrocketing. My weight dropped dangerously low. I was physically and emotionally weak, rundown, weary, and bent on alternately finding help and denying I needed any.

One Weary Patient

In February 2005 the trapdoor opened beneath the facade I'd carefully constructed from a series of false beliefs. The belief, for example, that if I ignored extreme physical symptoms, they didn't actually exist. The belief that if my body kept going, there was really nothing wrong with it. The belief that if I ignored my body, it would miraculously heal itself. These are the simple beliefs that got me through the day. Then there were the more complicated ideas: the notion that I existed separately from my body, for example, and that I could force that deteriorating form beyond its comfort points and it would continue to function purely because I willed it to.

When things came to a grinding halt, when I suddenly felt completely overwhelmed by the destruction of my ridiculous, intellectual insulation, I found myself sitting in a boxy, very white doctor's office on East Seventy-second Street, part of the Cornell Medical Center in Manhattan. I had made the appointment seeking help for my recently diagnosed osteoporosis.

I sat incredibly erect in an uncomfortable chair across a small, round table from a small, round endocrinologist—one of *New York Magazine*'s Top 100 Doctors—who said, looking over the rim of his half-glasses and without any intonation toward the melodramatic, "Unless you immediately gain ten pounds and begin a regimen of strength training, your bones will begin to spontaneously fracture by the time you're fifty."

That wasn't much more than ten years away. I staved the encroaching panic by going on the offensive.

"Look at me. My body's too weak for anything that rigorous or demanding."

"Your bones need this. Your body needs this. But I'm not just giving you advice, I'm telling you facts. You have advanced osteoporosis—early stages, but for someone your age this is critical. You don't have a choice. You must begin training with free weights if you hope to stop the progression of this disease."

He spoke sternly, but his eyes were warm, a trait I wasn't used to in doctors. It was distracting. I wanted to climb over the table and crawl into his lap and have him tell me everything was going to be okay.

This doctor hadn't been stumped enough to resent me, as the others seemed to. Instead, he drew charts and graphs and pictures of bones to explain what was happening inside my deceitful body. With great attention I watched him deftly draw upside down while quoting facts and figures from the National Institutes of Health. And then, as I often did, I left the present moment. I receded back somewhere in my mind, and from there I drifted away toward the future, where I pictured my tibia snapping as I stepped off the curb to cross York Avenue, an arm cracking as I lifted it to hail a cab, kneecaps shattering as I descended into the subway.

I imagined my life—currently curtailed by extreme fibromyalgia, escalating liver enzymes, muscle and joint pain, undiagnosable stomach and intestinal ailments—confined to home, bedridden. I would have to move back in with my parents. My life would be consumed by that sad grayness of life among the ill. I'd spend hours in bed, too exhausted for company. I'd see even more doctors and specialists. I'd never take another bike ride. I'd never travel abroad. I wouldn't get back to teaching. I'd never write another poem. I'd sink into inertia. Eventually, I wouldn't even have the strength to walk Baylee.

At some point I realized the doctor had been waiting for me to speak, so I looked back over his half-glasses and said, "I can't gain ten more pounds. It's taken me the past six months just to gain the nine I've put on. All this overeating is exhausting."

"I can't help you until you do," he replied, closing my file. "Don't make another appointment with me until you weigh 125."

I averted my eyes and stared hard at a spot on the carpet. I didn't want this doctor to see the welling of tears.

Some loss of consciousness happened the minute the endocrinologist gave his ultimatum. It's the same process that happened anytime some event triggered memory. Whenever I was faced with a medical choice for which I couldn't discern the safest option, my memory and emotion simultaneously unfurled, prompting physiological reactions I could not control—a panicky quickening of the pulse, a flip of the stomach, an unexpected shortness of breath, an increased awareness of the pounding of my heart, the muscles' urge to get up and run, a well of tears that left my mind fuzzy and unable to focus.

As the endocrinologist continued giving directions I could only hold my breath and watch him speak while the past crept into the present. My consciousness split, cleaving within itself, and I found myself navigating an increasing chaos while expertly feigning composure.

I stared at the carpet, then, with very controlled movements, I collected my things from the small table at which we sat—a *Newsweek* magazine I brought for the waiting room, a small notebook in which I kept copious notes about symptoms, prescriptions, treatments, a running log of questions I hoped some doctor would answer, a thick file of test results. The endocrinologist referred me to a nutritionist and suggested I add to my diet cans of liquid food, the same meals given to hospital patients through feeding tubes. I solemnly shook his hand and thanked him for his time, agreeing that I'd come back when I'd gotten myself up to 125 pounds. I smiled cheerfully, threw my bag over my shoulder, and forced myself to bounce out of his office. I joked with the nurse. I caught the elevator. I held my breath and ran out of the lobby into the freezing winter cold, where I burst into tears.

The sharp air caught in my throat. My chest heaved. Tears on my cheeks left small icy traces. People hurried by. They looked well fed. They looked stable. They did not look as if their bodies were out of control and they, struggling to get them back on course, were completely ineffective. I walked to the end of the block where a railing overlooked the East River. There I could, in privacy, completely break down. But when I stood, gripping the wrought iron, turning my face against the wind, the tears suddenly ran dry. The impulse to sob about all the years I'd been ill, all the subtle fears I'd carried since 1981, vanished. I was worn out by worry, sick of living a fearful existence. I was, I suddenly realized, sick of fear in every way it had crept into my life so that my body was its home, my mind its temple, my soul its prisoner.

I am afraid, I thought. *I have always been so very afraid.*

This was a new thought, an unexpected discovery, a revelation I turned over in my mouth like a piece of hard candy. Despite the list of fears I'd made, I had never thought of myself as a fearful person. But then I thought of how often I was afraid when there wasn't anything tangible to be afraid of. How often I felt fear in the hypothetical, and I suddenly realized: I carried fear around like a fetish.

"I am afraid," I said out loud with surprise and relief.

Fear had always felt so normal that I didn't usually notice it. On this day, however, I could see how, for the nearly twenty-five years since SJS, my life had revolved around fear: escaping it, accepting it, fighting it, reprimanding it, giving in to it, rebelling against it.

Leaning against the railing, listening to the city's sirens and car and truck horns, the human voices and shouts, anger suddenly surged through me. It wasn't fair so many lives continued moving forward while I stood in the freezing cold, paralyzed by fear and sadness. I tried to blame fate. But fate, like faith, likes neither to be pinned down nor burdened with human qualities. How, then, had I become so bound by fear? What held me to it? Out of the silence and blankness of my mind, the answer stepped forward with unwanted, unexpected clarity: I did. I did it by my continued habitual reaction to that long-ago crisis.

Suddenly I wondered if the heaviness I felt in my body and bones, the one I believed was symptomatic of some undiagnosable malady, might be due to (dare I say, created by?) the tremendous weight of the fear I carried in the muscles and bones and mind that lived through the illness. It occurred to me that my current inexplicable illness—and all those doctors' collective inability to help me—was the embodiment of my one greatest fear: I will fall ill with another mysterious sickness and no one will be able to help.

As I watched the river swirling below me, I felt a sudden new strength. I imagined I could be just like any of the people I saw on the street going about the day without being pushed from behind by fear. I imagined I could be just as functional and physically fit as that woman jogging by in her red scarf and mittens. My body, usually meek and lethargic, suddenly felt a capability for fitness. Who knew, maybe

I could even lift some weights.

Shivering from both the cold and a great sense of anticipation, I turned away from Queens and headed back toward York Avenue.

Today, I decided, *will be the day I begin to reclaim myself.*

Only one person could help me with such a task. I took out my cell phone and with clumsy, gloved fingers, dialed Greg's office. I hadn't seen him in three years.

"Greg!" I shouted against the wind and a passing siren. "I'm coming back to finish what we started!"

PART THREE:

CLARITY

Sanuk?

A s soon as Greg opens the door to his office and greets me with his lilting *Hello!* I know that I will effortlessly slide back into my blue chair, back into our relationship.

I have made a pact with myself that in one year I must be healthy and free, or else what I have always worried about—that I will become completely unhinged by an illness I had when I was thirteen—will be true. Since making this commitment, I feel myself unraveling faster and to a greater extent than ever. I flail around, grasping at any idea to cure my bones, my muscles, my blood, my GI tract, my liver. Hoping for positive results, I submit myself to every invasive test. Completely shut down I walk like a zombie into procedure after procedure. My parents are appalled at the ease with which I even consider an extremely painful liver biopsy that probably won't prove anything.

I've been managing only two hours of sleep a night for several months. With my worsening health, spontaneous crying jags become even more frequent. On street corners, in university hallways, in restaurant bathrooms. I feel composed, going about my routine, and then suddenly, my eyes fill with unstoppable tears.

In the middle of all this confusion, we take a family trip to see my grandmother in San Diego. Bret and I are sitting in a marina when he muses, "I wish I could have my boat in the water year-round."

A sensation of utter peace washes over me and I hear myself say, "You can. We could move to Florida."

For a long time I've fantasized about living by the beach. Especially lately the notion of heat, sand, and the healing presence of the ocean is very vivid in my mind. It's never occurred to me that my family might go, and I don't want to leave without them. In this moment it suddenly seems I might have a chance at persuading Bret to make the move.

"Everything about our lives and careers is transportable," I say. "You can manage money anywhere. I can teach anywhere. Let's do it."

It takes eight months to make the move. First, Bret and I fly to Palm Beach County to decide where we want to live. Palm Beach has a healthy financial community, which will be good for Bret and Dad to transfer their business. It also has more than fifteen colleges and universities, so I'll stand a good chance of being able to continue teaching. Our next task is convincing my parents to leave Scarsdale.

We tell them over dinner one night, "Sell the house and get in the car—we're moving to Florida!" They immediately agree. My parents are Southerners; they are ready to go back to their roots. Even Bret's girlfriend gets onboard. She and Bret fly to Florida and he buys a condominium on the beach. Through a local real estate agent, my parents and I arrange to rent townhouses so that we can decide later where we want a permanent residence.

By the time I start seeing Greg again, I have only four months left in New York. We work fast, three times a week or more, sometimes back-to-back sessions. Since the thought occurred to me that I could be free of fear, I want to snap my fingers, click my heels, do whatever it takes to make it gone. Reminding myself that I can redefine my identity becomes a sort of mantra. It's clear I need to reconstruct myself, but I don't know where to begin.

"Do you know the concept of *sanuk?*" Greg asks.

"Never heard of it."

"It's Thai for 'fun' or 'joy,' but the meaning goes beyond our American idea of those words. For the Thai, *sanuk* means finding something worthwhile and fulfilling in our lives. What would bring you *sanuk?*"

"I don't know... In order to be worthwhile, it would have to be something that tests me. Something fulfilling would prove to me how strong I can be, how adept I am at survival, and how worthy I am of surviving."

"That's not something that needs to be repeatedly proven, Michele. Personal worth never needs proving. It just is. It's a fact."

"I need something more solid than that. Each time I prove I still have the strength to survive, I prove the fact of myself to myself. I draw out and define an identity I can actually envision."

"And does that make you feel better?"

"It gives me a sense of reality. It helps me know who I am. It connects me to the earth, to the world, when in my head I actually feel like I'm orbiting in outer space. And that's on a good day. Most days I'm not even in my head. My body is here, and then there's me over there."

I hold up my right hand about a foot away from the right side of my face.

I pause for a moment to see how Greg takes this weird admission. When he looks nonplussed, I continue.

"Every test of myself confirms that other, incredibly strong person I became in the hospital was real, that she still exists, that I can be her when and if I need to be."

"Why don't you be her every day?"

"She's only for emergencies. I wouldn't know how to be her under normal circumstances."

"Is she that different from you?"

"She's more powerful than I am."

"But she is you…"

"I don't think my regular self could be that strong every day."

"How else is she different from you?"

"She's transcendent, and at peace, and…"

"Go on."

" . . . I have the sense she's bigger than I am. I can't explain it; she's just better than I could ever be."

"Do you like her?"

"Yes, of course I *like* her. I just can't *be* her. I don't feel capable of living up to who she is. It's like she's got this huge spirit and I'm only this little body, and there's no way she can fit in here."

"What would make you worthy of her?"

"I don't know. She frightens me."

And so it just rolls out of my mouth, the truth behind the truth of my fears, the reason I can't see myself: I am afraid of what I see. This girl who can resist death frightens me; this girl who can survive, who possesses a fierce and overwhelming internal power to transcend and endure and carry the heavy weight of the past, terrifies me.

But then Greg's right there, helping me move forward.

"Has holding on to this fear of this other self grounded you in a good life?"

"No, of course not."

"Perhaps it isn't being able to hold on to something that gives us the sense of self and personal worth we desire.

Maybe letting go of fear would give you more to hold on to in the end."

"But if I let go of those things, what will be familiar? If I let go of the identity I have salvaged from the wreckage of that experience, who will I be now?"

"Whom would you choose?"

"I have no idea."

It seems that each time Greg and I lay to rest one aspect of the past, another one pops up. I begin imagining myself still in therapy when I'm ninety, shuffling into the office on my walker. *When will we ever be through?* I ask Greg. And he enigmatically answers, *You'll know.*

So I push forward, week after week allowing Greg to force me into territory I previously resisted. We discover things about my fears and their origins. We discern where my mind needs to be realigned, where the subconscious has taken an idea and twisted it into negative and destructive beliefs. We begin to see where these self-sabotaging thoughts have taken root and also how to yank them out. I'm finally beginning to mount a serious defense.

Greg explains that the brain encodes experience in neural pathways and that in the case of life-threatening experience, those neural pathways can become overactive. Our goal is to "process out" the experience of my illness, severing these overactive neural pathways as we go along. We use information processing techniques: Eye Movement Desensitization and Reprocessing, Thought Field Therapy, Emotional Freedom Technique, and Tapas Acupressure Technique. As Greg moves his fingers in a pattern through the air, I follow them with my eyes. Or I tap meridian points on my face and body while repeating sentences prompted by Greg. Issue by painful issue, we process and reprocess aspects of my past.

Greg says the body knows things beyond the mind, and that sometimes the body knows more. So we pose questions to which we gauge my body's response by muscle testing. I hold my arm at a ninety-degree angle to my body. Greg places his palm on the top of my arm, just above the elbow. He asks me a question and presses down on my arm. The strength with which I resist allows us to assess the strength of what I believe, or the weakness. In a way, we read my mind according to my body's responses. Since I don't trust my body, and my mind always feels like an addled, unfocused mess, this method isn't easy for me to believe.

But I trust Greg, so I submit and am surprised that our sessions invigorate me with conscious and subconscious success. I develop a greater degree of ease in talking and feeling. I leave each session with optimism and rush back each time with the idea I will be rewarded, I will begin to gain weight, my body will become less fragile, my health will be restored through a sort of psychological witchcraft in which I cannot wait to engage. Little by little, the creaky machinery of the mind/body connection, which was shut down and boarded up so many years ago, begins to turn on a well-greased axis. I begin to recognize the existence of my instincts and where and how they reside in the reactions of my body. I begin to practice listening for and gauging the strength of that inner voice. I begin deferring to it on small, insignificant matters, like what route to take when I walk to FIT.

It's a stupid exercise, but it limbers my body and mind not to think but to act and react. I train myself to feel impulse and respond, no questions asked. Soon this sort of behavior becomes automatic, and I begin walking around feeling all warm and fuzzy with the thought that maybe, just maybe, there is a way to join back together my Before and After selves, my fear and my strength.

A Long, Slow Look

Greg and I make good progress. I feel a lightness where I'd previously been weighed down. But I still have a problem letting go of fear.

"Fear makes me feel like things are under control," I explain to Greg. "I'm always afraid, so I won't be shocked when something frightening happens. Or I'm always afraid, so I'll see something bad coming because I'm looking for it. In the past, whenever I've tried to let go of the fear, I feel lost. And then I feel frightened that I'm lost, until I find something to fear again and then, I feel better, more connected. Without fear I feel like something's missing. It's a ridiculous cycle, but I can't break it."

"You have to make the decision to break it. You're like the survivor of a shipwreck and you saved yourself by grasping onto a piece of driftwood, clinging to it until you finally reached shore. But now you're on dry land and you continue to carry around that piece of driftwood, even though it's no longer necessary and, in fact, it's doing you harm. Michele, you can spend your whole life standing on shore gripping your old piece of driftwood. Or you can empty your hands, take a walk on the beach, board another boat, and understand it is certain that if you were to be in another wreck and need to save yourself, that old piece of driftwood would be too waterlogged to help you survive."

"Fear feels necessary. It's a part of who I am now."

Greg shakes his head. "That's what you believe, and that belief makes you feel unique. We all want to feel original, but you're getting your sense of uniqueness from the wrong place. Holding on to fear and your 1981 experience keeps you separate from everyone, including yourself."

In these sessions it is not unusual for me to burst into tears. It seems I walk into Greg's office ready to instantly dissolve. Today, as my general optimism sinks into a specific fear that I will never be wholly well either psychologically or physically, I give in to the emotion and grab a handful of tissues from the box beside my chair.

"We're never going to be finished," I sob. "I'm never going to be free. I'm never really going to live in the present tense, outside of this fog I've moved through for twenty-four years."

"You will when you decide to." Greg's quiet confidence is like being wrapped in a heated blanket on a freezing winter night.

He continues, "Victor Frankl wrote that the ultimate freedom is what we have in our mind. He said 'the last of the human freedoms' is choosing our attitude in any given situation. If you continue to protect the fear in your mind instead of banishing it, you're right: You will never be free. But if you create a freedom in your mind—if you choose a different attitude—then you can accomplish what you want to do."

I crumple a tissue and stuff it into my handbag. Eventually, I stop the tears. I look at Greg and love his faith in me, and I want to rise up and be that woman he's suggesting. But it's almost the end of the session and all I can say is, "I want to, Greg, I really do. But I don't think I can do that today."

This work with Greg unsettles me. It's hard to concentrate. I go through end-of-semester motions at FIT, where I teach a full load of classes in 2005, but I live in my own world, circa 1981. It's exhausting and counterintuitive. Papers wait to be graded, final exams need to be given, panicked students ask for end-of-the-year counseling. And there's the question of my health, which continues to deteriorate, and to which I'm not paying much attention. I get second opinions without definitive answers. I survive each week by going to a homeopath who gives me a neon pink IV cocktail of strong vitamin potions that wires me with enough energy to fly through the next three days.

I engage a trainer who structures a very simple strength-training routine that I do three times a week. I am determined to reverse the osteoporosis and, while I feel incredibly weak, an enormous fear about my bones commits me to the program. Plus I'm binge-eating, trying to gain weight so the endocrinologist will agree to see me again. I sit down with a half-pound bag of roasted, salted cashews and finish it while watching Rachael Ray's latest episode of *30 Minute Meals* for inspiration. I bake a chocolate cake for my mother for Mother's Day and eat so much of it that I have to make another—and I don't even like chocolate. I gorge myself on all kinds of things I never eat, just to feel I'm taking proactive steps toward my own well-being. Since I began working with Greg, my digestion has settled enough for me to eat more in quantity for short spurts. I walk around with a stomachache most days because, poor stomach, it is appalled at how much I keep trying to stuff into it. My metabolism remains quick. The pounds cling slowly.

In this deeply confused and chaotic state, I decide after all these years to educate myself about SJS. Blocking out the past means I have no well-formed idea about the facts of my illness. One steamy July night I cautiously lower myself into the chair at my computer and Google 'Stevens-Johnson Syndrome'. A site with pictures of SJS patients comes up. I take a deep breath. I double-click on the link. I think I'm ready to see, from a clinical point of view, what SJS looks like.

I am wrong. At the first image I realize I'm making a terrible mistake. The graphic images of blistered, burn-ravaged bodies are like a fist sending my stomach up into my throat. I feel the urge to run. A scream tries to battle its way from behind my teeth. And right behind it, a sob tries to push through. I turn off the computer and sit on the edge of the chair until the simultaneous impulses to vomit and weep subside.

There are two weeks left before we make the move to Florida. I am busy packing up my life, but my inability to speak my own history or look at a few photos of some anonymous people gnaws at me. And so, one night in the sweltering heat with no air conditioning, surrounded by boxes, I sit down to face the computer again. But first I shut myself down emotionally. This is research; it isn't personal.

I go to the site for the Stevens-Johnson Syndrome Foundation. They have a page of pictures, but first, you have to proceed past a warning of their graphic nature. I take a deep, relaxing breath. I listen to the constant whir of traffic on the West Side Highway, the bark of a dog in the park across the street. I look at Baylee asleep on his back with his feet up on the wall in a corner of the room. The present is active and alive. I click my way into the past.

The images are beyond graphic. They are disgusting. They are men and women and children and a tiny infant in the worst moments of deep pain. A man holds his arm above his head and turns his face away from the camera. A woman looks miserably and angrily at the lens. A child slumps over and vacantly stares ahead.

I have to close the link.

But then the shock fades a little and I click the link again. This time I can make myself look because this is not me. This *was* me, but now I am fine. In this moment I am safe, and I force myself to take a long, slow look.

Palm Trees

Baylee and I spend our last night in Manhattan at the Hilton Hotel. At the end of the morning rush hour on August 2, 2005, we meet up with my parents and Bret and his girlfriend to make a three-car caravan. Shortly after 10 a.m. we drive through the Lincoln Tunnel for the last time. Baylee is strapped into the right rear passenger seat of my car. He sits serenely, like a Sphinx, looking at me with a sage expression of calm reserve. With each mile we cover I feel pieces of the past break free and tumble away. With every state line crossed I envision a fresh beginning, one in which my own history will not follow me. I imagine no longer being haunted by the past. I see myself moving toward a future in which I drop all pretenses and become real.

After three days of driving, we finally pass signs for Tallahassee and Daytona and Orlando. This final travel day, we drive the entire ride without stopping. I can barely contain myself. The closer we get to Palm Beach, the more something inside me continues to give way.

When we roll off I-95 onto exit 83 at Donald Ross Road, the last foundation of my facade finally cracks. I coast down the exit ramp and the feeling overwhelms me: *I am home.* The streets are empty and stretch before us in long, flat, three-laned, palm-tree-lined endlessness. We drive east toward the ocean. In August, South Florida evenings exist as individual moments between thunderstorms, and as we drive toward our new homes lightning flashes and rain spatters. I've got the windows open because I want to feel everything about this place. My new habitat, whose air bubbles with humidity. My new environment, whose scent is full of sea spray and palms. Where the sun sets in a mauve, thundercloud-covered sky. Where neon salmon streaks of sun fading in the firmament announce the melding of heaven and earth.

Without warning I begin to cry. Not silent tears brought on by an awesome respect for nature and the universe, but the sobbing heaves of some final relief as I roll into my new town where I have never suffered, where my past does not exist.

Later, in a rented butter-yellow, three-story townhouse, I fall into a deeper sleep than I have since I was a child. I sleep for an incredible twelve hours, roused the next morning only by the sound of palm fronds hitting the side of the house as they sway in the ever-present ocean breeze. It takes me a second to remember where I am. And then I wake a little more and remember I'm in Florida and I take a moment to lie in bed looking out the window, watching the palms, thinking, *I live where there are palm trees!*

Gradually, I become aware of an unfamiliar feeling I can't name, a sense of anticipation similar to what I used to feel when I was young and woke up on the morning of my birthday. I lie very still and let the feeling come to me. Soon the beginning of understanding moves like a porpoise cutting through water, swift and sure, clean and direct. I wait as a thought moves up from the depths, and then something breaks through, the recognition that I'm feeling something I haven't felt in twenty-four years. Slowly, I name it. I say out loud: *I feel at peace.*

It's the act of hearing the words that makes me remember the one thing that would induce this: yesterday I walked away from my past. I left behind the hospital and all the other accumulated landmarks of my anxious fear. Now I see before me only unfettered vastness—the endless straight and flat Florida roads, the endless rise of royal palms into the sky, the endless horizon at the edge of the ocean, the endless possibility the future is not replete with hidden obstacles waiting to trip up my survival.

For the first time since 1981, I feel free.

See, Learn, Know

My first month in Florida passes as a dream, literally. My physical state is so depleted I don't immediately look for a job. My parents offer to help me financially so I have space to heal. With my time my own, I sleep constantly. The days have a deliciously monotonous routine: I wake at sunrise and take Baylee for an early walk on the beach. I have breakfast. I take a nap. I do some reading. I have lunch. I take another nap. I read some more. I sleep again. For the first time I cook, planning recipes, shopping, and inviting Mom and Dad over for dinner. It's a time of peace and restoration. Gradually, my energy returns and I gain weight as the days flow by in an endless stream where the only thing that matters is each whim of my body being immediately satisfied.

Greg and I continue our work over the phone twice a week. We make progress. We break through the fear to a point where I begin to imagine for myself a different life than the invalid one I am used to. This happens oh, so slowly, but I hear the machinery grinding in my head. I fantasize I could be her, the girl of such vast energy I glimpsed for just a moment in the hospital. I imagine myself strong and free and vibrant and healthy and able to succeed without enduring the pitfalls of illness. One day, walking along the beach I feel myself as I would like to be: happy, unafraid, able to live without looking back, a strong source of joyful vitality. Over a period of weeks I sink into this freedom, this positivism, and, miraculously, my stomach calms so that I can eat without indigestion or bloating. My muscles lose that last burn and ache and feel rested and at peace. I sleep and sleep and sleep. Even more miraculously, this September my hair does not fall out; instead, it begins to grow dramatically. I watch in amazement as it becomes thick and full.

By mid-September I feel refreshed and a little disoriented, as someone coming out of a dream rejuvenates and slowly (a little unwillingly) remembers what had been on the mind before sleep. I'd like to report that moving to a new state does, in fact, abolish everything that was on your mind before the move. I'd like to confirm that you wake up in your new surroundings and nothing connects you to where or who you were before.

But in September the beast of the past comes out of hibernation and I return to the trenches of researching Stevens-Johnson Syndrome. I dive into the cold, hard facts and make some surprising discoveries.

First, I did not survive Stevens-Johnson Syndrome after all; I survived Toxic Epidermal Necrolysis Syndrome (TENS), the most advanced and lethal form of SJS. TENS kills forty to seventy percent of the patients it afflicts, usually because of poorly managed care that allows it to evolve into sepsis or other secondary problems. While records now reflect that SJS/TENS affects only one in 2 million people annually, the disorder wasn't well known in the early 1980s. Even today, its rareness causes it to be often misdiagnosed. Treatment protocol is sketchy at best. SJS/TENS has been described worldwide at all ages in all races, most frequently in women. Original symptoms, which appear one to three days after taking a medication, include but are not limited to rash, fever, general malaise, joint pain, bloodshot eyes, and blisters.

The offending medications can be as common as ibuprofen or as complex as a combination of sulfonamide and trimethoprim. Lesions begin symmetrically on the face and upper part of the torso and rapidly extend over the course of two to three days. A "Nikolsky" sign appears: the superficial layers of skin slip free from the lower layers with slight pressure. There are two types of TENS: the more usual is with spots, meaning that epidermal detachment is found in small, flat, unconnected blisters. TENS without spots also features epidermal detachment, but in large sheets. Clearly I had TENS without spots.

Frequent long-term effects include dry-eye syndrome; opthalmalogical scarring; corneal blisters, erosions, and holes; permanent skin damage; lesions on internal organs; asthma; diabetes; blindness; epidermal scarring and altered pigmentation. Complications can affect the skin, mucosal membrane, lungs, GI tract, and kidneys.

The key to effectively managing TENS is early detection and the immediate discontinuation of the offending medication. Steroids are often used in an attempt to lessen the severity of the reaction. Typically, Prednisone and Benadryl are given immediately. Sometimes this helps; sometimes not. Patients placed in burn units fare the best since those medical professionals are well educated in debriding skin and preventing infection. Patients are put on constant intravenous therapy to avert dehydration and to try to minimize weight loss. In extreme cases, the mouth, esophagus, and GI tract are so debilitated that patients can't swallow, risking further complications from an inadequate supply of calories. In severe cases, the mouth and GI tract are rendered unusable and an IV no longer affords enough nutrition, so a feeding tube is introduced.

I visit every website I can find. When I exhaust the Web, I turn to bound material. My first act as a Palm Beach County resident: getting my library card. I spend hours sitting in the reading room beneath a high ceiling with a bottle-glass window that every afternoon fills with light. I comb medical encyclopedias and journals for definitions and case studies. I suddenly have an unmitigated need to see and learn and know.

Slowly, the details fill themselves in and I build a reality of September 1981. Now I have facts to round out what I most remember: a feeling of great powerlessness and help-lessness, and the realization that I could not control the outcome; neither resistance nor escape was an option. Now, while I remember the struggle to cope, to be brave, to face each grotesque and pain-filled day with grace as I whim-pered, raged, and screamed, I begin to see the girl in the bed, naked and disfigured, her body as well as her soul bloody and weeping while she, so inexperienced in the art of survival, bobs on the alternating waves of giving in and struggling to survive.

I begin to see things in focus. The move to Florida stops the blur of my entire life. Florida in August, September, and October simply gets too hot for anything to move fast. Days are like statues standing motionless in the sun. Only the breeze moves as it floats off the Atlantic Ocean and over the dunes. Here, life unfolds in one-story, sedentary strip malls beneath a blue sky that lethargically extends forever and is, every night, full of countless, fixed stars. In this atmosphere it feels safe and easy to view myself. After researching TENS,

I move on to study the psychology of survival. Immediately, I recognize my advanced state of what the books call dissociation: "a perceived detachment of the mind from the emotional state or even from the body."

One day, toward the end of autumn, I look up trauma. It is like looking in a mirror.

Wound

The word *trauma*, I learn, dates back to the year 1656, when it entered the Greek lexicon as a word for "wound." It wasn't until 1889 that it entered the realm of psychology, and not until 1949 that it officially began to denote a psychological state. In medical terms, *trauma* refers to a serious bodily injury, wound, or shock. In the psychiatric realm, however, trauma is defined as an experience that is emotionally shocking and often results in lasting mental and physical effects.

Of course, people use it in much more casual ways. I remember a friend in college saying, *I was so traumatized,* referring to a compromising situation between herself, her boyfriend, and his ex-girlfriend. She meant she was embarrassed. Real trauma is much more serious. I was not embarrassed by what happened at the end of the summer I was thirteen. This is the first time I have ever associated my illness with its specific result on me. I have always viewed the aftereffects as coincidental, individual, and scattered.

Now, as I approach my thirty-eighth birthday and come to understand the overall concept of what happened, I want to know more. I start outlining and highlighting articles.

I write out facts on index cards. At the library I check out so many books with such frequency that I become friendly with the guy who runs the front desk. He's a student at Palm Beach County Community College.

"Are you taking a psych class?" he finally asks.

"No."

"Then what are you doing with all these books?"

"Research."

"For what?"

"I don't know."

"Cool," he says, nodding languidly. He pushes his horn-rimmed glasses farther up the bridge of his nose and tucks a stray dreadlock behind his ear, then shoves my pile of books toward me.

I hurry home with my stash: *Trauma and Recovery; The Stranger in the Mirror: Dissociation—The Hidden Epidemic; The Modular Brain.* I can't read enough in those categories that objectively render facts, hypotheses, tested opinions. These medical and other books give me an education I really don't want: Reflected in their pages, I see who I have become. I fill out a simple test in one of the books and discover I rate mildly on a trauma amnesiac scale, moderately on a depersonalization scale, and severely on the identity-confusion scale. I begin to feel a sense of belonging. Many of the books discuss the importance of integrating memories into the present identity. I join an SJS support group online and begin calling survivors to hear their stories.

In all of this reading, I learn about the mind/body connection; how the state of one can mirror and affect the other. I discover how that connection can present itself after trauma. I find a lot of examples among writers. For instance, for seven years after her friend's murder, Amy Tan woke up with laryngitis on every anniversary of his death. After the trauma of her rape, Alice Sebold developed migraines. During her affair with her father, Kathryn Harrison developed unexplained illness, asthma, and rashes. When the memories of her child sexual abuse resurfaced, Martha Beck's wrists mysteriously turned black and blue. I think back over the years and suddenly realize that every year my hair begins falling out on August 31, the day I entered the hospital. And it continues until the middle of September, when I was released to go home.

I am alone, lost in the labyrinth of memory and trauma, without answers to important questions: What happened to the thirteen-year-old girl I was before? Afterward, how did she become this flailing, invalid woman? Each day requires that I honor my trauma, and so I do. Each moment revolves around a sacred dedication to preserving the tragedy of a thirteen-year-old girl, and making sure the woman she becomes constantly validates the fact that she survived. Each day I test the strength of my mind and body to ensure that I continue to survive.

After years of this, it's no surprise I'm a mess. It seems memorializing one single event has led me to a life that does not celebrate my survival but makes me struggle for it every day. I exist, mostly, in my own head, struggling to deny memory by filling my mind with knowledge, education, and tasks. In situations outside my own inner dialogue, I am only half present, and even then through a fog.

The research, however, tells me all of this is normal. The books cite cases in which stress causes emotional and physical symptoms, plus erratic behavior. When looked at through this clinical focus, I recognize my own circumstance and can admit how extreme it has been and continues to be. I discover there is a clinical name for the state in which I function: Post-Traumatic Stress Disorder (PTSD). I take a self-test based on the Diagnostic and Statistical Manual's PTSD criteria and answer positively to twenty of the twenty-two questions. I call Greg for our weekly phone session. I lay out the facts.

"Do you think I have PTSD?"

"What is PTSD?" Greg asks.

"Post-Traumatic Stress Disorder. But I'm not sure the label applies to me. I don't have flashbacks all the time."

Greg agrees, and so it won't be until much later (when research leads me to meet with a psychotherapist, and then also a therapist who does PTSD assessments for the Veterans Administration) that I learn for sure the PTSD label most definitely applies to me. In the meantime, I proceed on intuition. I refuse to identify myself as someone who fits into this neat and disturbing category. I decide there must be another answer. I commit to more research. I take out more books from the library. I read day and night in the quest for another concept. But instead of finding less, I only find more and more and more of myself. Slowly, I accept the truth.

When I exhaust the library's resources, I turn to Barnes & Noble. I comb the shelves for books written by experts on trauma, survival, and identity. Gradually, it becomes a great relief to leave things in the hands of academics and professionals, to let them fashion modes of expression to explain me.

All this research makes me feel emboldened. I feel the itch to try formulating some linguistic mode of my own expression. I come to understand and then accept that I have been physically and psychologically traumatized, which makes me wonder why no one has ever pointed this out to me, or spoken about the past's effect on my present in quite this way. Why, for example, when I was thirteen and about to be released from the hospital, no one gave me a vocabulary for going forward. Why in the past twenty years none of the top doctors, psychiatrists, and therapists I've seen put together the trauma, the anorexia, the insomnia, the mysterious GI issues, the avoidance, the physical reactions to anything that reminds me of my illness, the hypervigilance and hyperarousal, the dissociation, the depression, the disconnect, the rage, the tears, the nightmares, the ever-present anxious fear. How is it possible PTSD could fly so below the radar when it was staring everyone in the face?

If the psychiatrist who spoke with me before I left the hospital had said, *You've been traumatized,* would I have responded? If she had said, *You survived and there's physical and psychological baggage that comes with that,* would I have turned to her and whispered, *More?* If Greg had said, *After trauma the mind can do strange things,* would I have answered, *Such as?* It's possible that had the hospital psychiatrist given me a name for what I experienced, some warning of what to look for if things began to unravel, I would have been able to stop the subsequent subtle disintegration that occurred. It's possible that had Greg been able to point out the obvious, I would have educated myself sooner.

It's possible, then, entirely possible, that I could have healed two decades ago.

Blank White Canvas

My father's favorite advice has always been, *Action puts fear to flight.* Whenever something unnerves us, we've been taught to meet it head-on and act as a force upon or against it rather than allow it to solely act against us. Between walks on Jupiter Beach, happy hour at the local tiki bar, and dates with Stuart, the owner of a Golden Retriever Baylee met in the dunes, I once again heed my father's words.

Socrates wrote that language is "an activity that moves the soul toward definition." Words can deliver us from our solitude, or deepen it. They are our most specific form of translating what exists in a heart through the landscape of a mind. I have always used language as a fence, as a guardrail *against* truth, definition, and exposure. So often my words have cloaked my self in disguises designed to ensure anonymity. Or, the lack of words has kept me separate from even myself. Recently, however, I sense the ability to use language in another way. I begin writing poetry again, starker poems and more to the point, writing more directly than ever about the aftereffects of illness and its consequence on identity.

I begin to feel safe. Somewhere, in the midst of unpacking in this rented space and over hours of phone therapy with Greg, plus the research, I understand the problem has been that I never acknowledged my past and then came back to the present. Instead, I have lived in the trauma and run away from myself in every moment. It is time to sit still.

Toward the end of October, I settle down to read *The Year of Magical Thinking* by Joan Didion. The book presents a parent's perspective of a child's grave illness, plus the death of a mate. Didion's book is a graceful, heartrending, and subtle description of illness, survival, powerlessness, and grief. I am glued to the couch with the book, on the verge of tears the whole time—not for what she and her family suffered, but for me and mine. I can't stop the slow sink into Didion's prose or my own recollections. The two fuse together like the collage inside a kaleidoscope.

As I read, my emotions come closer. I inhale Didion's

prose and my own anxiety, and an odd thing happens. In my mind I suddenly sense the existence of a staircase leading up to a door that opens into freedom. The more I read, the more courage I feel. I want to integrate the memories and tell my story. There must be some way to lay out the facts of the past, make sense of what happened, and understand how to heal. There must be a way to climb the stairs, open the door, and step into freedom.

During all this mental activity I've been house-hunting. I'm not good at making decisions. I feel overwhelmed by choices. I don't know how to prioritize, strategize, or recognize deciding factors. And I've never put down money for something I couldn't easily return. A house, especially in the rapidly peaking market of late 2005, will be impossible to get rid of if I make a mistake.

I call Ann, one of my Manhattan colleagues and friends. Ann recently bought an apartment overlooking Riverside Park. I figure she'll have some good advice about this kind of decision making.

"I don't know how to choose," I tell her. "I don't know what's important to consider."

As I knew she would, Ann immediately has an answer. "There's only one thing you need to think about."

"What's that?"

"If you were sick, would it be a nice place to be sick in?"

"That's it?"

"That's all you need to know. Would you be happy being sick there? That's the big question. That's how I've chosen every place I've ever bought."

I think about the house I like the most. It's a small, Spanish-style villa in a young gated community surrounding a lake. I envision the courtyard, the archways, the high ceilings, eggshell-colored walls, and sand-colored tiled living-room floor. I think about the many windows and how the light, streaming in from all directions, casts long and inviting swaths of sun on every surface. I think about how the architecture twists and curves. The house rambles with the same ease and flexibility of a slow walk through acres of cool woods. I imagine myself rambling. I imagine myself moving slowly from room to room. I imagine myself home.

"Yes, Ann. I would be happy being sick there."

"Well, darlin', there's your answer." I hear Ann take a long drag on a cigarette. "Buy the house."

I move into my permanent home on Valentine's Day 2006.

I continue burying myself in research because it provides a frame to my own experience. I read that in trauma victims it's pretty normal (almost routine) for some aspect of depersonalization—feelings of being detached from your body or mental processes—to occur. I feel better understanding why, since I was a teenager, I have felt so disconnected from myself. I am looking for a way to reforge the connection.

For weeks I read about identity: history, definition, foundation, debates. Starting with the ancient philosophers and working my way forward, I learn about the social, political, and economic factors that influence our understanding of the term. A concrete definition continues to evade scholars and philosophers. I've turned to the research, and even the scholars are lost.

Meanwhile, Greg and I keep making progress and then crash into a wall. It happens like this: One afternoon he asks, "How do you see yourself outside of your trauma?"

"You mean, who am I if not a survivor?"

"Yes. Describe yourself as if TENS is not something you experienced."

"That's impossible."

"Try."

"I can't do it."

Greg and I sit in silence. I try to make a picture in my head of what I would look like if TENS had not occurred. All I see is a blank white canvas. There is nothing, not even a small, modernistic black dot in the midst of all the white. Not even a starting point from which to sketch an identity without pain, fear, and suffering.

"I can't do it, Greg. I can't see myself at all."

"You're in a new place. You're starting a new life. Perhaps now would be a good time to try."

So I do try. At first, nothing works. A reimagination seems inconceivable and this disturbs me until things with Stuart get serious. He wants to marry me. He wants children. Nothing has changed since that day I decided I do not want kids. Nothing has changed, either, in my feelings about marriage. But when Stuart broaches these topics, I try them on— not because I love him, which I don't. I don't even really like him. Stuart is sweet but undependable, overly emotional, and I suspect that he lies. Still, I'm trying to warm up to the idea of being with him because I'm anxious to get on with redefining my life. One day I actually think to myself, *By this time next year, I could be married and pregnant.* And those ideas actually sound incredibly appealing just because they put a picture in the blank white space.

Wife and *mother* would certainly define me outside the boundaries of TENS. Maybe if I did something so opposite whom I feel myself to be, my whole life would just fall into place and I wouldn't have time to think about all this other stuff that obsesses me.

As enticing as it momentarily seems, though, marriage and motherhood are not for me, and neither, especially, is

Stuart. We split. I wander around Palm Beach County, pausing at odd moments to ask myself: *Who am I without TENS?*

At this point I become consumed with the idea of telling the whole story of my illness. I begin writing it down, carefully laying the scene, describing the details I remember. The past becomes all I think about and the only place I live. Several of my physical symptoms return. Insomnia starts up again. Depression descends like a curtain. I sink fast and far and deep.

Addicted

Around this time I accept a job offer from Bret and Dad to help them found a money management business. I have an easy job running the office. I don't take my work home with me. I spend all my free time writing, which isn't easy but I'm doing it. Of all the memories I work so hard to shelve and put away, the out-of-body vision threatens to overwhelm me. Finally, I manage to get it down. That's when awful, new nightmares begin. Up until this point the nightmares have always been that some faceless figure is trying to kill me while I attempt to escape. Now, it's not me in danger, but other people are dying, or one person I love is dying, or a person I barely know gasps one final breath while I run down streets screaming for help, or tenderly hold him or her in my arms begging for a little more time while I sob uncontrollably. All the dreams end the same way: everyone dies. I do not save one single person.

I awaken every morning worn out, anxious, defeated, depressed, and sleep-deprived. I'm up half the night because after a nightmare I can't fall back to sleep. I start getting up at 2 or 3 a.m. I read. I watch really bad television for two or three hours before going back to bed for an hour or two when the sun begins to rise. I don't go in to the office but hang around the house. I eat, and overeat, and walk Baylee, and take a nap, and call Bret to say I'll be in late.

Then I stumble upon Elizabeth Wurtzel's *More, Now Again: A Memoir of Addiction* and everything completely falls apart. Wurtzel doesn't control herself or her material in a frame of disciplined organization. She is out there and in your face and raw and emotional, writing about snorting forty pills of crushed Ritalin a day. Wurtzel and I should have nothing in common. I have never been on prescription drugs for mood problems. I have never used recreational drugs. I expect reading about Wurtzel's addiction to a medication prescribed to boost the effects of her antidepressant to feel entirely removed from me.

Only it isn't. Wurtzel writes about outrageous and self-destructive behavior, overwhelming emotion, the worried love of family and friends, the insane need to continue an obviously disastrous activity, obsession, and compulsion. Her language is personal and infused with such sad honesty it immediately draws me in. I don't even feel it happening, but on the third page Wurtzel writes, "My whole life is about the next five minutes," and I recognize that feeling. We're both compensating for not being able to control something. She can't handle her present; I can't handle my past. The need to prove I remain invincible, impervious, stronger-than-all-of-you-put-together drives me the same way she feels bound to pluck all the hair out of her legs with a tweezer. She manages every moment by getting high; I manage every moment by engaging in a hypervigilant micromanagement that makes me sure I will see the danger coming and be prepared.

With Wurtzel's book, however, I don't see the danger coming. It hits me hard over the head and shocks me. The two days it takes me to read the book strip me of all pretenses and haul me into an empty room with a stark white light, where I am forced to observe addiction at its basest level. Wurtzel's story directs me to notice the universal elements of obsession, and I realize, with heartbreaking clarity: I'm an addict, too. I have a trauma addiction and it has, over the course of the past twenty-five years, repeatedly threatened to kill me. Even though on some level I have known this danger for a long time, I keep coming back for one more hit. As I come to terms with this information, a weird sensation of reality descends. It explains the depression and the survival mechanisms and the coping and the cycle of getting better and then sabotaging it.

Everything I've been trying to deny and/or fabricate into truth floods me with a relentless, unbearable honesty. I'm more devoted than ever to writing it all down, and more paralyzed, too. Writing seems like the only thing that can save me, and also the thing promising to destroy me. Writing without the veil of dissociation, writing sober as it were, will be the test of my endurance. I'm not sure I'm up to the task.

It does feel good to tag those memories and emotions and cage them in the confines of one-inch margins. But also, it doesn't feel so good. I wake up every day dreading the task of all this writing even while I feel compelled by a frightening fanaticism. It's incredibly, horrifically difficult to even turn on my computer, but now I've been programmed. I walk zombie-like into my home office—and then I can't sit down. I circle my desk. I keep forgetting things I need from other rooms. I lie on the couch for a while and wait until the moment feels just right to begin. I turn on the computer, I open the file, I watch the blinking cursor—and then I go back to lying on the couch overcome by anxiety. And then I eat something. And then I bake something. And then I eat what I've baked until I've stuffed all that anxiety down my throat and I can finally sit down for two or three hours and ride several waves of nausea while I attempt to give all this amorphous stuff a language of its own.

I am frightened of what more will be lost if I heal. And what will be found: a woman I don't recognize, will possibly never understand; a life engineered entirely by confusion.

It's comforting that things are beginning to make sense, but now I don't know how to proceed. I decide I need to cut off all communication with Greg.

"There's a battle going on within me," I tell him. "A really fierce war between my Before and After selves. This is it. This is the end. One must win, and one must lose. I have to sit back and let them fight it out. I can't do this with you involved. That's too many people in too small a space."

"Call me if you need me," Greg replies. And just like that I am on my own.

My sense is that the key to my After self winning this war has to do with my ability to construct some sort of clear, post-trauma identity. I'm still not sure what actually defines an identity, or how one would deliberately create it, so once again, I turn to the literature. Most of what I read centers on the idea of a quality of sameness in an individual over the course of a life. I do most of my research at night sitting on a chaise on the balcony outside my bedroom. While Baylee scampers back and forth barking a warning to anyone who walks by, I attempt to make a list of what qualities characterize me Before and After TENS. Immediately, I get stumped. I don't remember much Before. I have snatches of impressions but nothing that seems evocative of an entire self. Afterward there exists only the feeling I'd better keep my world small, not too many possibilities, so that things at all times remain under control.

I know now that prompt trauma recovery requires a number of conditions in order to be successful, conditions that need to be implemented between two weeks and four months after the trauma. On my own, I didn't know how to make any psychological conversion either soon after or years after my illness. I still don't know.

All of these hypotheses and facts toss me into deeper chaos. I wander in an entirely unknown galaxy. The stress of all this recognition, reconstruction, and disorientation causes my hair to fall out faster than ever and it's not even September. It begins one day in March when I find my hands full of strands—not the average fifty that fall out in the course of a day, but more like 250 by 8 a.m., with the whole day to go. I continue researching and writing and suffering more frequent nightmares and not sleeping at all, so that three months later so much hair is gone that I need to buy a new bunch of wide headbands and tiny hair clips to conceal the amount of scalp that shows through the thinning strands. I feel embarrassed and self-conscious and pitiful-looking. I've gone from not worrying about my hair—for the first time since college, actually, not constantly checking to see how obviously it has thinned out or grown in—to positioning myself in front of the mirror first thing in the morning and last thing at night so I can turn around and around to view the balding damage from every angle.

And then one day I wake up to see that on the right side of my head, one-third of the hair is just gone. It's a Monday morning. The hair was there last week, I'm sure of it. The hair was there last night. But now there is an enormous, gaping bald spot. I am mesmerized by the empty space. I can't stop fingering it. The scalp is soft and a little sticky and creepy to touch. My fingers worry over the exposed skin, back and forth in an effort to feel some sort of fuzz, some sort of promised growth, but there is nothing—absolutely nothing—there.

I Need to Dance

The summer crawls by as I research and then write page after page, pouring my story into an organized form, seeking the answers that will set me free. Autumn continues my obsession. I drive myself to continue writing despite the negative impact because I am convinced this single act will bring me to freedom. Slowly, my hair regrows. The bald spot now possesses a layer of fuzz.

Observing the toll this project takes on me, my mother frequently suggests that I stop writing. I try leaving the computer shut down but then feel so lost that I write more in an effort to stave off panic. I am terrified I will never be well. I press forward and then find myself such an emotional wreck that I burst into tears in the middle of a massive New Year's Eve party at the fabulous Breakers hotel. I can't get outside of my head for even this one night.

I grab my brother's hand. "Let's dance!" I say, and pull him into the crowd. On the dance floor my body relaxes and my mind suspends until I become only the feeling of every dance, only a soaring, swelling experience of freedom coursing through me as my body melds with each note. Something strange is happening. I am waking from a very long, deep sleep. The phrases of music are luring me back to consciousness. I want to run and leap and shout and laugh and sing. I feel an exorbitant *joy.* Suddenly it occurs to me:

I might free myself from the past by feeling more of this joy in the present.

It is after midnight; 2007 has begun. I decide that by my fortieth birthday, a little over a year away, I will replace this bogged-down fear and depression with the thousand unbound effects of joy. In order to do this I will need to find a way to bring more of this joy into my life. I will need to dance. A lot.

New Year's Eve remains on my mind as life resumes its post-holiday routine. I decide I need at least a weekly dose of joy. One Saturday night Bret and I make plans to go to Noche, a new local restaurant and nightclub. Decorated in bronzes and golds with soft yellow lighting, the place is both trendy and homey, with a fireplace that divides the lounge from the dining room. Friday and Saturday nights a DJ plays everything from 70s disco to Top 40 to rock.

Francisco, the gorgeous Latin lover-looking maitre d', seats us at a table beside the dance floor.

"The perfect table so that later you can dance, no?" He winks as he holds out my chair.

Bret and I order a smothering amount of tapas and are just finishing when the DJ appears and music suddenly erupts.

A few people immediately step onto the dance floor. The clientele is older and wealthy. They wear Chanel suits and cultured pearls, Brioni ties and Gucci loafers. Their generation doesn't really know how to freestyle. Like my parents, they learned to dance at sock hops, so mostly they do a sort of East Coast Swing, no matter what type of music. After a minute or two of watching, Bret and I can no longer sit still.

Within an hour the crowd becomes younger. Hipsters in their thirties and forties take up residence at the bar. They wander around the space. They lean against the walls sipping mojitos and observing the dance floor.

I get caught up in the music and the freedom and the flow of unstructured movement. That familiar energy surges through me the minute Bret and I begin to dance. Music enters my body through my feet and squirrels up my limbs and spine through my neck into my head, where it whirs around like a mental massage, releasing an explosive endorphin.

A huge smile involuntarily curves my lips. I'm free and cheerful and content. I'm feeling sexy and divine. I'm rocking my hips and shaking my ass and feeling invincible. I own the floor. I'm some kind of fabulous. I am good out here!

And then they arrive. Two women and two men. One woman is lithe and petite. She wears a black skirt about calf-length and a black tank top. The other woman is taller, a little plump. She wears an unflattering black wrap dress and a basic black pair of shoes that are round-toed and low-heeled with a T-strap across the ankle. The men both sport black pants and black button-down shirts. One couple looks American; the other looks Latino. All four look unremarkable and uninspiring and self-contained; they do not blend with the crowd, which is chic and self-conscious and uncomfortable.

These four people come to the edge of the dance floor. They do not, as most people do, stand and survey the crowd. They do not study the geography of the floor as if looking for a place to slip in. They advance like a small battalion, sure-footed and disciplined. Then the women turn toward the men, the men hold out a hand, the women place their palms inside the offered hands, and the four of them step onto a corner of the dance floor and begin to dance—not like the rest of us are dancing, but really dance. The song is a disco which, in the world of dance, translates to a hustle.

These two women syncopate and turn and hip-swivel. The men lead them through their moves with a simple rotation of the arm, a soft caress of the shoulder, and the women spin around and around. These couples glide over their small corner of the floor with grace and uninhibited ease. While the rest of us are stomping and shoulder-shifting and bouncing in place, these couples move around each other with the energy of tightly coiled springs.

The men are styling, their hands and arms perfectly placed, but it is the women who capture my attention. Both are incredibly light on their feet. The illusion is that they are skating over the wooden floor following an undetectable lead. There is no obvious communication between the partners, yet they dance flawlessly. They are a synchronized extension of the music. Bret and I take a break. We sit at our table, faces flushed and moist with sweat.

"Watch them," I say, pointing to the two couples.

Bret turns and observes. The Latino leads his partner into five successive spins. She comes out perfectly on the beat without looking the slightest bit dizzy.

A small voice in me whispers, *I want . . .*

"Cool," Bret says, nodding his head.

The man leads her into a dip and then out into a diva walk. She is wonderful and fluid and beautiful.

As we continue watching, the small voice. . . *I want . . .* becomes louder and louder until it erupts from my lips. "I want to dance like that!" I shout over the music.

"You could!" Bret answers.

"I want to be that good. I want to look like her," I say, pointing to the taller, plumper dancer. She moves with an unusual ease in her body. Her face is focused but at peace. There is a genuine softness to her movements, as if she sinks into each step as an afterthought and expects to land against a feather pillow. A small smile plays at the edges of her lips as if she harbors a secret only her partner might guess.

"I want to look like that," I continue saying aloud to myself. "I want to be able to dance like that."

Somewhere in the pit of my stomach a small coil of joy has begun to stand up like a snake being charmed in a basket. It hums and thrums and writhes. It is a very small sensation, but I sense its great desire and potential to grow. I steal a peek at the two couples again and again. Each time I do, the coil in my stomach tightens and springs. I watch them spin and wrap, and I understand that there is something I can do to get closer to this.

PART FOUR:

HEALING

Light As a Feather

My first dance instructor is Flavius, a Bulgarian émigré who somehow ended up at the dance studio near my house. The studio is run by Blanche and Walter, a professionally ranked wife-and-husband dance champion team. They are a very outgoing pair with quick, professional smiles trained to perform the minute you enter the studio. From Austria, Blanche is tall and dark, sinewy and severe. She looks as if she could crush you with the heel of her dance shoe and not think twice about it. Walter's Scottish background makes him light and open-faced, a good visual balance for his wife. They have no children, but their Chihuahua runs around the studio barking and tripping the dancers and peeing on the dance floor.

Flavius is smaller than both Blanche and Walter. Lithe and taut, he's about five feet nine inches tall with close-cropped wiry brown hair and a loud, gravelly voice. Flavius is only twenty-nine, but he looks a decade older. He is professional at all times, brusque but kind. He and his lover/dance partner, Georgette, still compete on the international dance scene.

My first lesson with Flavius is not, technically speaking, my very first ballroom lesson. When I was nine my mother enrolled me for a year in Miss Covington's School of Dance. Every Thursday afternoon I put on a nice party dress, my squeaky, black patent leather Mary Janes, and a small pair of white gloves. Then I spent two hours learning to waltz and fox-trot and cha-cha with a bunch of other little people. My proudest moment came when a guest instructor visited the class and, after watching all of us, pulled me out of the lineup to demonstrate the waltz.

"You're so light on your feet!" he exclaimed. "Light as a feather. Wonderful."

Now, thirty years later, Flavius leads me into a rumba. I have absolutely no idea what I'm doing.

"Rumba is the first dance everyone learns. It is the easiest," Flavius says as he shows me the basic pattern. "It is just a simple box step. The tempo is: quick, quick, slow." It's a sexy sort of flirtation dance in a slow and sensual style.

Flavius and I go through the motions for a few stilted, rusty moments and then he says, "Stop leading."

"I'm sorry. I grew up leading my brother. It's a habit."

"Well, you've got to break it. And loosen your hands. You are squeezing so hard. Now, lift your arm from the shoulder. Don't keep lifting your shoulder. Your shoulders should be relaxed and far below your ears. And your feet should be grounded on the floor. Why are you on your tiptoes? Dance flat on your feet."

I try to keep up. I try to move and step the way Flavius does. I think I am doing a good job. Actually, I think I am doing a phenomenal job. We're moving around and around in a square and I think I am, indeed, light as a feather.

"Loosen your hips, Michele." Flavius's thick accent cuts through my reverie. "Let them move with the natural force of the dance. Let the hips make a small figure eight. Like this. Good. Now, bend and straighten the knees."

I watch Flavius and then make a conscious effort to let my hips roll from side to side. I get into the motion. I step.

I bend one knee. I straighten the other. I bring my feet together. I roll my hips. I'm dancing and think I'm doing well enough for someone who really does not know what she's doing, until Flavius stops dancing and says, "Stand still. Listen to the music. How do you hear the beat?"

"What do you mean, how do I hear the beat?"

Flavius points to his ear. "How do you hear it?"

I put my hand up to my own ear. "The same way you do. I hear it. I feel it. Why?"

"Because you're not on it."

Not on the beat? I *know* how to follow a beat!

But I don't say this to Flavius. Instead I say, "Oh…."

"What you are doing, this being ahead of the beat, this is common with people learning to dance. It's not to worry. Being ahead of the beat is just you not feeling comfortable. You will see, the steps and the movement will come. But you must also listen to the music when you dance. It is not all about the steps. It is about interpreting the music through the steps. We'll try again."

And so I begin the awkward task of trying to get my head and feet to work in tandem. I try to find the beat, listen for its rhythm, interpret it in my body, remember the pattern of steps, react to Flavius's stiff upper-body lead and pull it all together into some semblance of dance. But I am not used to being in a proper dance embrace. I am not used to being told what to do. I am not used to someone else controlling my every move.

"Quick, quick, slow," Flavius chants over and over.

Quick, quick, slow, I repeat in my head. *Quick, quick, slow.* And I try to get my feet to step in this sort of rhythm. Sometimes they do; sometimes they don't. I look down to watch my feet to see if they're doing what my head thinks they ought to.

"Don't look down!" Flavius corrects me. "You dance with your head up, always."

"I just want to see—"

"No!"

When I concentrate on the steps, I forget about the posture. When I think about the posture, I forget about the steps. But when I don't think at all, when I just give in to Flavius's lead, I am flawless, and then I get surprised that I've executed something properly, and then I realize I'm dancing—and just when I think I'm getting good I lose the beat, collapse my posture, and trip all over myself.

After about the fourth time of this cycle, Flavius sighs and says, "I think the problem is you don't believe you can do it right the first time. But you can. It's unusual, and rarely happens, but every so often there is someone who just immediately gets the steps. You are that person, but you don't trust yourself. So you think about it and you ask a lot of questions when the truth is, you did it perfectly the very first time."

This, of course, boosts my ego and makes me believe I will do great things on the dance floor. My prowess will shock everyone. I will stun and rock and burn up the floor at Noche! This idea provides enough motivation for me. I buckle down and seriously focus, but no matter how hard I try or how much I want to be, I am so very far from perfect. Flavius and I work on the same simple move again and again and again, until he says, "That's enough for tonight."

I leave the studio, and it doesn't matter that I have stepped on Flavius's feet and repeatedly erred. I feel high and exuberant. *I have been dancing!*

When I get home I bring Baylee outside and while he sits and surveys the universe from our driveway, I practice the basic rumba box step under the light of a streetlamp.

Balance, Center, Line

I hear music and feel a response to the primal, heartbeat-like rhythm. I make an individual expression to a universal sound. I imagine learning ballroom dance will be all the fun of freestyling with only a little more structure. I am completely wrong. Ballroom isn't about the fun freedom of bodily expression; ballroom is work.

Over the next few weeks Flavius and I settle into a genial relationship. We break the ice and joke around and laugh a lot as I attempt to stop leading and step smaller and loosen my grip and keep my shoulders down and my chest up and remember every piece of Flavius's technical advice, all the while following his lead, stepping in the pattern, and hearing the beat. It's enough multitasking to drive anyone crazy. Gestures and movements must be tightly controlled. They are not supposed to be wide and loose or as big as I feel them.

There's a lot of submission going on. I must submit to Flavius's lead, and my body must submit to my mind, which means the unconscious impulse must submit to the conscious command, which means the Ego is way involved, which makes things a tad more leaden in the transcendence department. Now, my mind decides and judges in every moment how large, how small, how tight, how loose—and my body must comply. My body doesn't like this arrangement. When there's music, it is conditioned to having its way and it's not giving up this freedom easily. My mind decrees, "Take smaller steps," and my body, caught up in the freedom of the music and the natural rise and fall of rhythm, pretends not to hear and lunges backward, cresting the wave of sound and throwing Flavius completely off balance, so that the move we are trying to execute drastically fails. I apologize countless times every hour.

I go to the studio once, sometimes twice, a week. I schedule my lessons at night, when there's only me and maybe one other student, which gives Flavius and me more space to work. I strap on my dance shoes (a beige Latin pair with three-inch heels) and join Flavius on the floor.

"Tonight, we're going to work on your turns," he says at the beginning of my fifth lesson.

Inward groan. My turns are sloppy and unbalanced, no matter how hard I try to make them otherwise.

"In dancing, the three most important things are balance, center, and line." Flavius stops our warm-up dance and makes me stand still and very erect. He ticks off points on his fingers.

"You must keep yourself balanced. You must hold yourself over the center of your body. You must at all times maintain the vertical line of your body. Nose over toes. This will make your dancing more controlled and shaped. Balance. Center. Line. You must remember these three things."

This is a lot of information. I have trouble assimilating it. I'm not sure I really understand it. To make matters worse, I'm not a visual person. Watching Flavius's illustration of each topic isn't enough to get me going. I can't see something and then mimic it. I end up with an endless stream of questions that lead to explanations that lead to more questions. I consume half the lesson with talking and watching Flavius's creative efforts at examples. In discussing the technique of a spin, Flavius finally resorts to placing a water bottle on the floor to demonstrate the idea of vortex and how dancers use it.

From the very first lesson, learning to dance is making me very humble. I have had to admit I am not the great dancer I perceived myself to be. I am not the star pupil I had hoped to become, either. I am just an average person who wants to learn to partner-dance and is struggling with even the most basic concepts.

I'm learning, too (and this might be the most difficult thing so far), the idea that sometimes it's better not to think. I have to let go of control. I have to trust my partner. I must let my body act on its own and trust that it knows what it's doing. This is a new idea for me. Another thing I'm learning is the discipline of patience, which I haven't had a lick of for any number of years. I've become the sort of woman who wants it all done correctly now, which means I am determined to force my body to do what I want, even while it, equally forcefully, refuses to comply.

Slowly, it's beginning to dawn on me that in order to dance as well as I want to, I must modify parts of my personality. I cannot be so centered in my mind if I want to allow my body to perform. I cannot be desperate to progress quickly if I want the slow evolution of technique to look professional.

Flavius and I continue to practice a simple turn where we both circle while executing the basic rumba pattern. I cannot get my body to slow down, to allow Flavius to act and then myself to react, so I step ahead of the beat and my balance is poor and I fall out of frame and that pulls Flavius out of the pattern and we have to stop, realign, and begin again.

"You are looking very serious," Flavius observes. "You will learn. Give yourself some time. It takes six months to a year before the muscles automatically know what to do."

Why did this look so easy when I watched those

couples at Noche?

"The best way to develop your own balance," Flavius instructs, "is to keep your sternum forward and your pelvis tucked. Your left arm should open out and then come in as you make the turn. Tighten up your movements—they're too loose."

I try to stick out my chest, suck in my abs, and generally tighten my body, all while staring at a spot on Flavius's forehead. I'm so taut I can barely move.

"Don't forget to breathe," he reminds me.

I expel my breath and shake my head.

"This will take some practice," he says. "You have to have patience, Michele. Dancing is not an involuntary activity. It must be learned."

I smile. "Sure," I say. "We have plenty of time."

But inside I'm thinking, *I want to dance NOW!*

Taking My Time

I'm trying to make myself slow down. Dance movements need to be precise. You need to track your feet on the floor. Even when you're taking a step, the ball of the foot should slide along the floor, marking the path over which your foot travels. Ballroom dancing is about elegance and quiet drama and poise. All of these things require a certain slowness of speed.

But I'm not sure I can move at slower speeds. Inside my head everything always moves at warp speed. I translate that into my body, pushing it to do just about anything in the name of efficiency. I am fast and furious as a racecar and

I like it that way. Unfortunately, in order to dance well, I am going to have to develop and finesse a great number of moves and techniques. I make a conscious effort to slow down everywhere. I try to relinquish: the habit of perfectly timing everything down to the second, of walking so fast down the beach, of trying to talk quickly, read quickly, write quickly. I try not to feel the momentum of individual minutes and instead feel the general, steady passing of an entire day. I try to walk more slowly, too, even if it's just down the aisles in the supermarket. I shop for lettuce and tomatoes and bananas while slowly pointing my toes and sliding my feet along the floor of the produce department.

I am exhausted all the time, and depressed. Still, even if I do nothing productive the rest of the day, I commit to my dance lesson. As soon as I step into the studio, another self emerges. My headache, lethargy, and heaviness in my limbs evaporate as some other persona momentarily takes control.

When I enter the studio for my next lesson, Blanche swoops over to give me one of her big, arms-outstretched hugs.

"Michele! You have to come to the mini-competition at The Isles. It's not expensive, only $300 to register and that includes a dinner dance, the competition, and a plaque. Sh! Sh! I know what you are going to say, but you are ready. It's just down the street and it will give you a good feel for what competition is like." She hands me an application and a few sheets of marketing material. "Say you'll go. We're all going together."

"All of us! It will be fun!" Flavius calls from across the room.

I can't help it. I want to belong. I want to please. I want everyone to be happy with me. I want to participate in the dance world. Also, every time I'm in the studio Blanche and Flavius tell me—before, during, and after each lesson—that I'm a wonderful dancer. Maybe I am ready to strut my stuff.

"Okay!" I agree.

Blanche flings her arms around my neck and gives me another great hug.

"Wonderful! Now you will have an objective to work toward."

"This will be terrific," Flavius says, and runs over to hug me.

I'm all caught up in the moment of these wonderful hugs, but there is a little part of me muttering that learning to dance, period, is really quite enough of an objective.

Flavius and I warm up with East Coast Swing. In order to devise a dance that was easily learned by people who were not professional dancers, Arthur Murray teachers stripped down and adapted the complex swing form into something the general public could accomplish. In the ballroom a street dance turned into East Coast Swing.

I am immediately good at it. It is extremely simple, with a 6-count basic step that can be quickened or slowed according to the music; there's single-, double-, and triple-step swing, so you can dance the same basic pattern to almost any swing rhythm. Flavius and I practice triple-step swing, which is done to a fun, fast beat. Because the music sort of mimics my own internal landscape—a little jittery, a little quick, but not maniacal—I easily hit the 1 & 2, 3 & 4, 5-6 pattern that lays itself out in a sequence to the right, to the left, backward rock step. In this dance there's no worrying about being ahead of the beat, there's no tangling up trying to bend and straighten the knee or move the hips in a figure eight. This is just good old perky American fun with a speeded-up "slow, slow, quick, quick" movement—and it's all over the floor. I love it.

Occasionally, I do lack the ability to follow, which prompts Flavius to say with sarcastic bluntness, "It would be good if you let me lead." But generally, this is a dance I can do with a great deal of proficiency, so that we cover a lot of ground in a short amount of time. After thirty minutes we have successfully executed the basic step, a cuddle hold, underarm turn, crossover turn, hitch kick, and a walk and kick. I'm feeling pretty savvy when we switch to rumba. I'm flying on a high dose of expert dance aptitude—and I am immediately humbled.

"Follow the curves of the movement by reflecting those curves in your posture," Flavius says. He wants me to begin shaping my body to add that extra layer of ballroom elegance. I arch sideways as I rotate in an underarm turn. I feel stupid. I look like the letter C. "Okay, not so much," Flavius responds.

Things go downhill from there. While in swing I am always on the beat, in the slower rumba I am always ahead of it. While in swing I can turn as an extension of the swing motion itself, in rumba I am stilted and wobbly. My body wants to *Go!* My muscles want to *Move!* They fight every second with my mind's decision we should wait, we should proceed slowly. The resulting motion is jerky and spastic.

Walter watches a portion of my rumba struggle. At the end of the lesson, he says, "Congratulations! You're doing very well."

"My turns—"

"Have patience. Turns are difficult. It's a matter of cultivating balance. That will come with time. You'll see."

It turns out he's right. There will be a night or a day or an hour or a move when, somewhere dancing with someone, for absolutely no reason at all something clicks and suddenly the mind and body understand each other and the dance goes so well that something magical occurs: As if it is nothing at all, you accidentally perform perfectly something you've been struggling with for weeks. This is what happens to me the next Friday night when I've finally worked up the courage to attend a group class at the studio.

I'm dancing with Seth, a twenty-eight-year-old Treasury Department Fraud Investigator. He's tall and very well built and wears a small pair of wire-rimmed glasses. An ex-Airborne in the Army, he still sports a crew cut of Brilloish black hair. His posture is that of an enlisted man, even though he's out of uniform in jeans and a blue flannel shirt. He's just relocated from Washington, DC.

From the beginning of my lessons I've been struck by that weird aspect of where to look while dancing with a partner. Over the weeks with Flavius, I've gotten used to looking directly at him so I can read his responses to my efforts. Now though, as Seth and I assume the open ballroom embrace and begin to practice the basic rumba step, I just don't know: Do I stare straight at his mouth, which is eye level? Over his shoulder? At the top of his forehead? I look at his eyes. I smile. I feel uncomfortable and look away. Eventually, I can't stand the silence and all the looking around so while we dance, I converse.

"Why did you decide to learn to dance?"

"Because I'm such a meathead," Seth answers, and this small sentence causes him to botch the step. We reassume the starting pose and begin again while he tries to complete his answer. "I wanted to do something that wasn't a meathead thing." He messes up the pattern again and we readjust and start over while he continues his explanation. "I just told Blanche, 'Sign me up for the biggest package,' and here I am. My first lesson was yesterday."

This makes me feel very safe. If Seth's first lesson was yesterday, he will not really know what he's doing, which means he won't really be able to tell if I don't know what I'm doing.

"I can't talk and dance," he apologizes.

We stop talking and concentrate on our rumba. Seth cannot remember the sequence of the four-step pattern, so I help him piece it together. I teach him. This is a change of pace for me. I like it.

The class switches to ballroom tango, and Seth and I relax. Neither of us knows what we're doing, so we vamp it up with a great amount of funny drama that leaves us laughing more than dancing. And maybe this is why something about turns finally clicks. Unlike with Flavius, with Seth I'm not trying to be perfect or get it right. With Seth, I'm just having fun dancing and when I do that, he leads me into the same sort of underarm rumba turn Flavius has been leading me into for weeks, and I execute it perfectly! I can't believe it. I make Seth lead it over and over, and every time I get it right.

For the rest of the night, I'm loose and easy to lead. I cha-cha with Walter and fox-trot with Flavius and swing with Seth and hustle with a stranger and about halfway through the party that follows the group class I realize, I'm dancing!

Salsa Freak

After such a turning point of an evening, I'm feeling a little bold. Maybe I don't need to wait any longer before

I get out on a real dance floor. One night after work I corral Bret and we go to Noche.

On Thursdays the average age at Noche's bar is sixty-five, but they're a rowdy, randy bunch. Regardless of birth-date, there is a fierce but genial meat-market mentality and an interesting energy. Where strictly younger crowds supply an atmosphere tinged with a predatory energy, the older generation provides an atmosphere that is more fun, less vulturistic, and more anything-goes, as if they know, 'If not you, I'll find somebody else,' and so there's no animosity or aggression. Eighty-year-old men wander through the crowd flirting, winking, and drinking. If I leave Bret alone for five minutes, pretty, wealthy, beautifully dressed and bejeweled women in their fifties crowd around, sniffing out this younger man.

Bret and I prop ourselves on barstools and take a look at the crowd, moving to the tunes of a fabulous Latin band. I watch no one in particular; my eye roves over the moving bodies. There are a lot of intertwined arms and turns and repetitions of the basic pattern. Salsa is a fun dance to watch. I'm studying all the dancers and listening to the music and soaking it all in when I see him. There is a guy on the dance floor and he is dancing the most amazing salsa. He looks Latino, but his skin is a sallow sort of white, his brown hair short and curly, and his eyes have the lazy, droopy dreami-ness of a close-to-the-equator climate. He's about my age and his feet move faster than my eyes can follow. His arms are in constant motion leading his partner into one pretzel-like move after another. His hips roll while his torso shifts in time to the beat. The dance floor is packed with Ameri-cans and Latinos, but I can't take my eyes off this one man. I stand by the dance floor for a better view and remain there for almost half an hour. The Salsa Freak (as I affectionately dub him) switches partners as often as the band switches songs. He never, ever comes off the floor. He smiles and laughs and sparkles with happiness and dance confidence. I must dance with him.

The problem is, I don't know how to salsa. I'm feeling simultaneously shy because of this and emboldened by my recent success with Seth. I finally muster all my courage and when a song ends and the Freak looks for a new partner, I make a beeline for him. He grins and nods and the music begins to play, but it's not a salsa. I don't know what this is; instead of the rolling jazzlike rhythm of salsa, this has a more militant staccato beat. The Salsa Freak pulls me into a very, very close embrace. I feel my eyes open wider as I stand face to face with him and say, "I don't recognize this music."

"Merengue," he says with a grin.

I struggle to make some distance between us, but he holds me so our hips connect and our bellies are pressed against each other.

"I don't know merengue."

"You don't need to know," the Freak says. "Just smile and hold on."

So that's what I do. He begins to move his hips from side to side in time to the fast beat; I have no choice, my hips move with him. Our bellies mash against each other as the Freak and I move sideways to the left, then sideways to the right, shifting our weight in a marching sort of step in each direction. When we get proficient at this basic movement, he leads me through some turns. I begin understanding the rhythm and the movements of the dance. The tempo demands a fun, boppy sort of rhythm. This is a fast dance without drama or shaping. I love it.

So I step and drag my feet and the Freak is smiling and I am smiling as he twists my arms into a pretzel-like shape and then magically untwists them without letting go. I'm feeling the beat and understanding the music and trying to give in and let the Freak do with me what he will. I don't know what I'm doing, but I am definitely dancing, and the Freak seems pleased. He nods and whirls me around in a full body embrace. Then he releases one hand so I can turn, at my own pace, beneath his arm. I'm getting into it now, my hips are shifting and I'm smiling and when he pulls me back into the original close embrace, I go with it and try not to mind that his hands, cloaked in the cape of a dance move, are gliding down my sides from beneath my armpits all the way over the swell of my hips. It feels wrong, it just does, to let a stranger do this, but then I look at his face and his expression is not lascivious. He's not even thinking about me, he's just dancing. He's like a physician and mine is just another in a long stream of bodies beneath his palms.

Just as I'm really getting comfortable, the music ends. I return to Bret at the bar.

"Hey! You looked great out there!"

"I didn't know what I was doing."

"You looked like you did. You got in some good hip movement."

"I just tried to follow."

I turn to watch the Freak with a new partner and realize I learned something tonight: I learned not to be afraid. Dance cannot be accomplished or understood standing on the sidelines or hanging around a studio. Dance must be attempted in the outside world, where the music is not the slowed tempo that studios teach to, but the fast pace of reality where you leave your comfort zone to dance with and among strangers whose developed abilities challenge you to refine and advance your own.

The band takes a break and the DJ takes over. He plays

a bunch of songs from the 80s and the tenor of the dance floor changes. A few of the Latin dancers remain, but mostly the crowd shifts to freestyle dancers. Bret and I get out there and relax into the routine of the familiar. The DJ plays Journey's *Don't Stop Believin'* and the crowd sings a raucous rendition of the chorus. It's late. People are tipsy. Everyone on the dance floor laughs and smiles.

I'm back in my comfort zone, but I have done the merengue and I have had the courage to go belly to belly with a stranger and now, while I'm freestyling and singing with Bret, there it is again, that little coil of joy, snaking up its head a little farther this time to get a better look around.

Stalling

Dance lessons and the pursuit of joy aside, I continue sitting down a few hours each day, sorting through the research and memories, trying to find some way to put it all into some kind of chronology that will make me feel at peace. I am committed to working things out by my fortieth birthday, eleven months away.

I try to write quickly, but the faster I work, the more frequent and intense are the nightmares. My insomnia and disquiet and unrest mount and build. I'm exhausted and weary. Living with my symptoms in a state of avoidance and numbness was so much easier than facing the past and feeling the emotions that erupt. I look forward to my lessons with Flavius as the only time that gets me completely away from all this angst. For weeks I leave the dance studio on a joy high, but after my eighth lesson, things change when

I announce my decision not to participate in the mini-competition after all.

Blanche pouts. "I wouldn't suggest you do anything you're not ready for or won't enjoy."

Flavius does his best to persuade me, and when he can't, he gets annoyed.

"You have some thoughts in your head and I don't agree with them, but that's all right," he says, and shrugs in that way someone arguing shrugs to let you know you're just not important enough for him to continue. Which makes me immediately continue.

"Flavi, it isn't economical for me to spend three hundred dollars when I'm not good enough yet."

He turns back to the stereo. "Fine."

But it isn't fine. Flavius is cool and detached.

He insists I wear a shoulder brace in order to teach my shoulders to relax. Despite my best effort over the past weeks, they continue to hunch up below my ears whenever I forget to monitor them.

I slip my shoulders into and my arms over the brace. It sits on my neck like a yoke. It's uncomfortable and I feel there should be two pails swinging from either end of the brace.

Flavius introduces me to the basic pattern for fox-trot. It is, as most dances are, another variation on the "slow, slow, quick, quick" pattern. I don't like it. Your head is held at a perfect eleven o'clock angle and you stand off to the left of your partner's center. The whole thing is too precise and not much fun, and the brace is driving me nuts.

"Enough!" I shrug off the brace, then say, "Let's do something fun. Let's do something Latin. Teach me salsa."

Flavius demonstrates in a slow, exaggerated pattern. "Salsa is danced on an 8 count: 1, 2, 3—5, 6, 7. You do not step but hold on the 4 and the 8."

We practice this with music for a few minutes. Flavius has slowed the tempo way down so I can learn to hear the beat. It isn't coming easily. When it seems I've got the basic step, he stops dancing.

"The first thing you need to learn, after the basic pattern, is to isolate your movements," he says. "Watch this." He faces me, his large eyes growing larger. One at a time he wiggles his right ear, then his left. "Can you do that?"

"No, but I can raise one eyebrow." I demonstrate.

"Good!" he says. "Now watch this." Flavius holds his body completely still and shifts only his ribcage from side to side. "You try it."

I do, and my hips go side to side instead. Flavius puts his hands on my hips.

"The hips stay still. Try again."

I think about moving my ribcage, but I awkwardly and uncomfortably rock my shoulders side to side.

"This takes some practice," Flavius says. "And patience."

Flavius and I spend a lot of time trying to help me find a way to isolate my ribcage. By the time I leave the studio, I can almost do it.

But things are never the same after that night. In refusing to compete, I have bucked the standard student path. As my ten-lesson contract draws to a close, I stall because I'm not sure I want to continue to learn in this environment. My refusal to sign a new contract irritates Blanche and Flavius, and they attempt to force me into formulating a program. It is unacceptable for me to just come in and dance, to work on whatever dance I feel like in that moment.

Instead of feeling joy during a lesson, I feel pressured and stressed with the strain of defining boundaries. Dance continues to be the only activity I can find to charm the snake of joy, and the more I continue to write—the more the nightmares occur and my hair continues to shed—the more important it becomes to find some light to balance the darkness. If I can't do that with Flavius, I will have to find somewhere else to go.

Tango

Exactly eight minutes from my house, the Ritz Ballroom sits in the L of yet another strip mall on Indiantown Road, one of the main thoroughfares in Jupiter. The studio can hold about eighty people. Mirrors line two walls, and around the perimeter of the room chairs and small round tables covered in a champagne-colored lamé cloth (which matches the valances on the windows) create a low-key, cabaret atmosphere for the weekly dances. There's a bar in one corner that serves double time as the DJ booth.

I walk into the Ritz at 8 p.m. on a Wednesday night in April. I don't know a soul. No one is expecting me. No one runs over to give me a hug. No one immediately welcomes or brings me into the studio for a look around or suggests I sign a contract. In fact, no one seems to care that I've appeared just in time for the group salsa class. Scattered around the ballroom about fifteen dancers, men and women from their thirties to fifties, strap on dance shoes. Their faces are animated. Laughter and voices fill the room with a blunt happiness. At the front of the studio a young woman in her twenties with long blonde hair collects money from her seat behind a large metal desk. I pay my $10 for the hour-long class.

"You're new," says the woman.

"Yes."

"Have you ever salsa'd before?"

"Not really."

"Well, then, tonight you'll learn. My name's Lisa. I'll be teaching the class." Lisa leans over the desk to shake my hand.

And that's it. She doesn't ask when I want to schedule my first private lesson. She doesn't quiz me about competitions. She just wants to know if I've ever salsa'd before, as if my intention in this moment is all that matters. I love the Ritz already.

The salsa class becomes fairly large, about twenty-five people each week. This is a good size for a group class—enough people to rotate partners and really get a feel for following different leads, yet small enough to become very comfortable with every one of your classmates. Lisa is a professional modern dancer and choreographer. She perfected her salsa by dating a Colombian, so she teaches a sort of club-style version of the dance.

As a warmup, Lisa leads us through a practice of the basic steps and then teaches one figure she pieces together from about five individual moves. We rotate partners, but I eventually partner up with a guy named Olaf. He's Norwegian, about ten years younger than I am, and sells luxury boats. He's new to the area and temporarily living with his aunt in a condo. She and her boyfriend brought him to class so he could "get out and meet some people." But if you saw Olaf, you'd know what I mean when I say it doesn't look like he'd have any problem developing a social life. He's got that great, smooth Nordic face with lustrous, long, sandy-colored hair and oceanic blue eyes. His smile reveals a row of small, perfect white teeth. He looks shy and demure, but when the music begins he's got great Latin hip motion and he can really keep the beat.

Throughout the month of April the class laughs a lot together and becomes a cohesive group. Several of us hang out in the parking lot talking for an hour after the lesson ends. Or, on the spur of the moment, we go disco dancing at a bar down the street. We develop a working knowledge of each other's lives. I become particularly friendly with a woman named Janet. She looks out for me during class. When I'm not sure what I'm doing, she's right there, sage and soft-spoken, giving me advice and showing me how to execute a move. In her fifties, Janet looks like she's just reached forty. She frosts her short black hair with orange-red highlights and keeps her body trim and fit. Janet attends group classes at the Ritz four nights a week.

"Dancing is like therapy for me," she explains at the end of class one evening. "And I need a lot of therapy!"

"Why?" The question just pops out. I shouldn't ask, but since dance feels like therapy to me, too, I can't suppress my curiosity.

"About a year ago, around the time I turned fifty-four, I realized my life lacked passion. I thought, 'Either I'm super-content or something's missing.' I discovered something was missing."

This answer makes sense to me. Something has been missing for me, too.

After our fourth class together, Janet suggests I attend the Argentine tango class at the Ritz on Thursday nights. I'm curious enough to try it out. When I walk in, four couples are already warming up. They dance around the room and although I'm watching very closely, I cannot pick out a steady, repeated pattern. Each couple is doing something different and in a different tempo and to a different time, and the men are walking or standing still and the women are swiveling forward or swiveling backward, or the couple is swiveling together and I can't see what the lead is for any of it or how the women know to do any step. At the same time, the mystery and beauty of the dance draws me in.

"Welcome!" A small man who looks like Robert Duvall's bowlegged younger brother with thinning red hair scurries toward me.

"You're here for Argentine tango!"

I nod.

"Wonderful. I'm Lewis. Have you ever done Argentine tango before?"

I shake my head.

"No problem, no problem. We'll teach you."

The class assembles in a circle and we introduce ourselves. It's all very cozy. It almost feels like an AA meeting and I want to say, "Hi, my name is Michele, and I've never tangoed before." There's another young girl in her twenties who is also a complete novice. When the class regulars see the new faces, they are very welcoming. An older gentleman with sagging eyes and jowls leans over to me and says, "I'll help you out. I'll be teaching you the basics. He," and he gestures toward Lewis, "only works with the young, pretty girls."

I search his face to see if he's joking, but his eyes are completely innocent. He really did just imply I am old and ugly.

"Thanks, I guess," I say.

"No problem, don't mention it. It's my pleasure."

But when the class begins, Lewis pairs me with someone else, someone who's been so quiet I haven't noticed him. He's a guy about my age with lanky brown hair hanging into cheerful brown eyes with lashes so long they curl up at the end. His eyes are set in a broad, round face with a perfectly straight nose. He has the sort of flat cheekbones that hint at some small degree of Native American heritage and skin that is smooth and tan.

"This is John, my assistant," Lewis introduces. "He'll be working with you tonight. Teach her the basic step," he instructs. "Just the eight-count pattern. Don't do anything fancy."

John nods and smiles at me. "Are you ready?"

"I don't know. This looks complicated."

"You'll be fine."

John leads me into a corner of the studio so we can work separately from the class. "The basic pattern for Argentine tango is an eight-count figure," he explains. "While most dances operate on the box system—their basic patterns form a four-count box on the floor—Argentine tango makes more of a rectangle by using eight steps."

Ugh. This is already too much math for me. But John breaks down the pattern into five steps and three steps, and it seems pretty manageable. He stands beside me to demonstrate the sequence. Side by side we practice. John's right: It's not so tough when I can watch him and follow his movements.

When it seems I'm fairly comfortable with the pattern, John suggests we try it in an embrace. We assume the classic ballroom open embrace, and then John adjusts to hold me a little more closely.

"The embrace for Argentine tango is more intimate than the other ballroom dances," he explains.

Indeed. John is about four inches taller than I; he leans his head down until our faces are level and separated by only an inch. His eyes are intense and impish and merry and so full of happy life, I'm completely distracted looking into them. I forget I don't like being this close to a stranger. I pitch my head a little toward him and return his smile. When we are settled in the embrace, John leads me into the basic pattern. We dance holding each other's gaze.

Forward, to the side, glide back, cross the ankles. John's right, this is easy! We flow around and around the rectangle. John's lead is gentle yet solid. He neither pushes nor pulls me around the floor, but lightly suggests where he wants me to go. My body follows him like a dog follows the hand holding a slab of meat; it's an instinctual reaction. I'm not following with my head because I know the steps, but with my body because my body is inexplicably drawn toward this body leading it. While I don't have a vast dance experience, I've already learned enough to know that John's lead is sort of magical. I've never felt something so loose and yet directed, so supple and yet commanding. We get good enough at the basic pattern that we begin to do it faster.

Suddenly, John moves his hand on my back so that I swivel backward. I'm not really sure what I'm doing. I'm not really sure what he's done, but something in his touch has made my body respond and now my feet are just trying to keep up. I think I am doing what those couples were practicing at the beginning of class, and I'm throwing my body into it because the move looked so pretty and professional. I'm just getting the hang of it when Lewis appears and barks at us, "No *ochos!* I just want you to practice the basic pattern. Show me the basic," he commands.

We execute it flawlessly, but Lewis shakes his head.

"Slow down, both of you. Michele, your feet should caress the floor. You're picking up your feet with almost every other step. Caress the floor. Slide the feet. I want your toes pointed down at all times and gliding along the surface. And take longer steps. Extend the leg, especially going backward. Extend from the hip. On each step you should feel your kneecaps as they pass each other. Brush the knees. Brush. The knees." He shakes a finger at John. "Just the basics. Nothing fancy. I mean it. No *ochos*."

John and I revert to the basic pattern. I extend my legs. I brush my knees. I caress the floor. Really slowly.

At the end of the class, as we're taking off our dance shoes, John overhears me telling Janet how much I love the Latin band at Noche on Thursday nights.

"Salsa is my favorite dance," John says. "Do you want to go to Noche after class next week?"

"Sure," I say. I'm a little taken aback. I've never had a guy ask me out when there hasn't been some flirting between us. John is completely affable, not flirtatious. There doesn't seem to be any hidden agenda with him. He really does just seem to be asking me to dance.

"Next week, then," he says, and walks away.

Just before I leave the studio, I go behind the bar to get a glass of water. John comes over and puts a scrap of paper on the bar before me.

"Here's my phone number. If you want to salsa tomorrow night, I'll take you to the best Latin club in West Palm Beach. Good night." John gives me a big smile and walks away.

I have absolutely no intention of calling him. I would never drive off to some unknown nightclub with a stranger— no matter how well he dances, no matter how much my body just instinctively wants to follow him.

The next afternoon, however, I find myself looking at the scrap of yellow paper with his name scribbled on it. I impulsively call and agree to meet at Coco Bongo at 11 p.m.

On and Off the Beat

I arrive at Coco Bongo ten minutes early, so I go in alone. I am immediately enchanted. The place is a dancer's paradise. The music is clear and crisp and infuses the space with sound. The ceiling is high, so the music travels around instead of being trapped down by the floor in a body-thumping, overly bassed beat. Next to the DJ booth on the far back wall hangs a single large video screen, currently filled with the image of a Latin singer. Along the sides of the very large room are long, rectangular bars, and against the front wall are small cabaret tables on an elevated level. Then I see the pièce de résistance: the sunken wooden dance floor. I've never seen such a beautiful homage to dance. The wood is a light, highly polished redwood that shines in the dim illumination. All around the perimeter of the square floor, an iron railing protects the sacredness of the dance space. This club understands that dancers must be set apart and embraced.

Nothing gets started in the Latin club world before midnight. At 11 p.m. there are only two couples on the floor. I sit at the bar and watch. The couples are both Latin, and their salsa is sensuous and extremely creative with many embellishments. While the Noche crowd (with the exception of the Freak) does the basic pattern in mind-numbing repetition, these couples are putting together figure after figure and adding taps and kicks to accentuate the music's natural pauses and accelerations. This dance is sinewy and playful, sexy and romantic. I'm completely engrossed in the show when out of the shadows a figure walks toward me.

I'm nearsighted and hardly ever wear my glasses; rather

than see details, I'm accustomed to discerning shapes. I can see that the figure approaching me is a man. He walks swiftly, with the poise and feline grace of a professional dancer. His hair is wet and slicked back and shines softly when light falls upon it. He dresses all in black: a tight black short-sleeved shirt that defines the muscles of his chest and arms, a simple pair of black pants. The square planes of his cheekbones give his face a rugged look. He carries himself with an air of simple and relaxed confidence; he's got ego but won't push it in your face. I am immediately attracted. I wait expectantly as he advances toward me. In the darkness I see the sudden white of a smile, I smell cologne. Finally, he stands directly in front of me so I can clearly see his face. It's John.

Gone is the sweet-looking guy with hair hanging in his eyes. Vanished is my tango tutor wearing a faded old shirt and a pair of khakis. Here is someone else entirely; someone multilayered and intriguing. I am shocked to be filled with the sudden impulse to leap off the barstool and throw myself in his arms.

My reaction to John is purely instinctual. Instead of my head, it is my body that (as it did in class) wants to be near him. I can't understand or explain it; this isn't a simple sexual urge. This is the flutter of something else, of an impulse flowing through my veins and pumping through my heart a barely contained excitement. I've never felt this before.

John stands in front of me and offers his hand, palm up. I control my desire to jump him and instead daintily place my fingers in his. I slide off the barstool and follow him onto the sunken dance floor. I'm feeling excited and thrilled and proud to take my place among the dancers. *I* am at a Latin club. *I* am going to salsa on this beautiful floor, with these beautiful dancers.

There are a few more couples on the floor now, all Latin,

all dancing the most wonderful salsa. John maneuvers us to an open space. He turns to me and we easily assume an open embrace. He begins to dance and, God, he looks like all the Latin dancers: sensuous and fluid and sexily macho, moving his body as if his bones are soft and malleable and the music is coursing up through his feet to the top of his head and then back down again. I imagine I myself will look like that, so I throw myself into the salsa and it is here, in the middle of this incredible dance floor, surrounded by these great dancers, across from this terrifically sexy and accomplished dancer whom I really, really want to impress, that I am suddenly appalled and amazed and dismayed to discover: I cannot salsa. Not one single, little bit.

I step backward and do the basic. I count: 1, 2, 3—5, 6, 7. But something is horribly wrong. The music is too fast. I hear too many beats. I'm overwhelmed by the cacophony of sound. It is as if someone has put a 33⅓ record on 78 rpm. I keep trying to catch up and start over, but I can't and my feet are getting off even their own rhythm and John is dancing and I'm shuffling and looking at him and wondering what the hell has happened.

I stop dancing and start over. I am so far out of sync that I step forward at the same time as John, which causes us to bump into each other and me to step on his foot. I am embarrassed and feeling utterly idiotic. I want the song to end so I can run off the floor. I stutter through the extremely long five minutes of music, still trying to smile and not look like I want to sink into the floor and hide. When the song ends, John mercifully guides me behind the railing.

"I don't know what's wrong!" I shout to him over the music. "In class I can salsa. Really, I can! I'm sorry."

"It's no problem; you just have to listen for a while. I was the same way when I was getting started."

171

"How long ago was that?"

"Eight years. Don't worry; it won't take you that long. Watch the other dancers. Your body just needs to learn to go through the motions faster than you're used to."

We stand against the railing overlooking the floor. The club is crowded now and the dance floor is packed with a sea of rhythmic bodies. Everyone makes eye contact and laughs and dances around and past and through each other. Although many are strangers to each other, the dancers are connected through a passion for the music and dance.

We watch through one song, and then another, and another. John points out a woman who is particularly wonderful. Her eyes are closed and her body moves of its own accord to the music. She has long brown hair that sways and a smooth flow from foot to foot. Her turns are fluid and precise; all her movements seem natural and unplanned, and her embellishments perfectly complement her partner's moves. They are an incredible pair to watch. She is very pale and Russian-looking, while he is the epitome of a Cuban. I study them for a while and then steal a peek at John. He is intently watching another couple and although we're standing in place, John's feet are constantly moving. A little timidly I try to imitate him, to find the beat and keep it in place, but I can't do it and I get flustered and just when I'm beginning to think we won't dance for the rest of the night, the music switches to bachata and, *aaaaaah,* I am in my element.

I love bachata music. It is light and fun and romantic and slightly Caribbean, so it almost seems the ghost of a steel drum hovers behind the predominant acoustic guitar. Best of all, the beat is easily discernible and simple to mark. It is the one dance never taught in any classes, but Lisa took five extra minutes at the end of class one night to line us all up and teach the basic step.

Excitedly, I turn to John and say, "I can dance to this!"

Again, he offers his hand. I take it, and he leads me to the dance floor.

The one thing Lisa did not cover in class is the bachata club embrace. Bachata can be danced with partners facing each other and holding hands between them, but that's not the traditional club style. I am completely unprepared when John pulls me tightly against his body. Our chests, bellies, and hips press together, and my right leg fits between his legs so I am, pretty much, positioned on John's right thigh. His arms wrap around me and I find myself exactly where I wanted to be when he walked into the club: enveloped by him. I wrap my left arm over his shoulder and my right arm around his neck and bury my face against his and close my eyes and in a second we are dancing and it is perfect. I follow John's smooth and fluid lead flawlessly. Our bodies perfectly synchronize and we're on the beat without any mishaps. The floor fills. We are surrounded by a dozen couples while our hips make a lovely Latin motion and our legs move in tandem and we spin around and around and the music plays sexily and with great romance.

The DJ segues a set of four bachatas and then rolls right into a set of merengue, so John and I are on the floor for a long time before another salsa comes on and I stumble through it. John patiently shows me the steps, counting them out for me, leading me into only the most simple figures. We muddle through one more song before we decide to take a break.

Thus, my salsa education begins. Throughout the evening John and I alternate between dancing and watching from the railing. The loudness of the music makes talking difficult, but there is an easy flow of communication between us. When John puts his arm around my waist and leans over my shoulder to point out a dancer on the floor, it seems completely normal for him to touch me, as if we have known each other for a very long time.

At 3:30 a.m. we finally leave the club. As we approach the exit, I stop to take off my dance shoes, but before I can bend down there is John, on one knee, unbuckling the left shoe and then the right and then, cupping each shin in his palm, slipping off one shoe and then the other. When he stands up I am struck dumb, staring at him. This is, without a doubt, the most chivalrous gesture anyone has ever bestowed upon me.

I don't know what to say except the totally inadequate, "Thank you."

"You're welcome," he smiles, and holds the door open for me.

Once we step outside, John does not touch me. Whereas walking around the club his arm wound lazily around my waist, now he walks me to my car with feet, not inches, between us. I talk and try to catch his eye, but he focuses on the path toward my car, which, when we reach it, he opens for me to get in. I'm mystified. In the club I thought we had a connection. I thought the good-night kiss was a foregone conclusion. But now here we are in the parking lot, totally alone, and—nothing. Not even the slightest bit of flirtation coming from him. In fact, John seems completely detached and uninterested in me as he holds open the car door. Since I don't know what else to do, I get in. John hands me my shoes.

"Good night," he says, and shuts the door.

Then he walks away into the shadows of the night, while I sit in my car watching him go.

Some Other Self

The more I dance, the less I care about the past. The more I dance, the more I feel joy, the more generous I become with myself, the more I live in the present, the more I let myself off the trauma hook, the less important the past becomes. Perhaps defining a self begins with simply making the first choice, simply rising up and deciding what you desire, and then methodically, like writing, putting one word after the other until you have created a whole self and a whole life in the process.

Alone at home, I sit still long enough to allow a pure, undocumented perception to rise to the surface. It is not, as I would have expected, an impression of fear or sadness. It is, instead, a calm, settled confidence. I don't know where it comes from, or to what it is attached, but I like sitting with it. I like knowing beyond the angst breathes some other self.

The only way I can develop this self faster is to engage with it every night. And so, like Janet, dance becomes my therapy. I stop writing and start dancing every night of the week. When John's not available, I go out with other friends I've made at the Ritz. Every morning I wake up looking forward to that night's dose of joy. I get out of my head, into my body, further and further away from writing and closer and closer to becoming a decent dancer. All this practice loosens up my body, so I feel it begin flowing with, rather than against, the music. The constant repetition helps my salsa evolve so that after two months I'm far from perfect, but at least I look like I belong on the dance floor.

While my dancing continues to progress, however, things remain static with John. I've never felt such joy as

I feel when we dance together. We walk into any of these clubs and my stomach starts to flip. When the music surrounds us and he takes my hand and leads me to the dance floor and we assume an embrace and we begin to dance, I feel transcendent and joyful and free. It's exquisite.

Still, John keeps his distance. We have great chemistry on the dance floor—each week, our connection becomes more and more intense as I become a more adept dancer—but off the dance floor there are absolutely no sparks. At the end of every night he removes my dance shoes, walks me to my car, and sends me home without so much as a peck on the cheek.

Then, just as I resign myself to being strictly ballroom, John does something interesting. We are at Noche, where the dance floor's thin layer of uncushioned wood is laid over the room's original tile. Nothing about this arrangement considers the comfort of the dancers' feet. By the end of the night the balls of my feet, balancing my body in three-inch heels, shriek from the abuse of kicking, tapping, and stepping on this unforgiving floor. At 2 a.m. one night, I limp off the dance floor and out onto Noche's back patio.

"Oh, my feet," I moan as John removes my shoes. I can barely walk and gingerly hop from one foot to the other.

"What's wrong?"

"They huuuurrrtttt."

"Come this way." John motions me to follow him.

Noche sits in a strip mall much nicer than most. The design of the peach-colored buildings resembles an Italian piazza, with fountains and foliage and lots of little nooks and side alleys. The buildings form a U shape around a marina where several large yachts lodge in their slips. John ducks down a pathway between two buildings and leads me to a bench overlooking the Intracoastal. A slight breeze drifts and I can hear the water slapping against the pilings.

"Sit here." John indicates the top of the back of a bench. I climb up and perch on it, and he sits beside me on the seat. He reaches over and tenderly takes my left foot in his hand. "Where does it hurt?"

"Everywhere."

"Okay," he murmurs.

"Mostly here." I point out the ball of the foot.

"All right."

John doesn't say another word, but soothingly uses every inch of his fingers and palms to massage and unknot the tension in my foot. His hands feel wonderful on my skin. They are just the right size to commandingly hold my foot without swallowing it. His warm and smooth fingers pulse with energy. The fact that for the first time John touches me for a personal, not dance-related, reason makes the moment feel electric.

Although this man does not seem romantically interested in me at all, I wonder if he's aware that gliding his thumb up and down the center of my foot is entirely erotic. I wonder if he smells the night-blooming jasmine and hears the boats rocking and sees the three-quarter moon shining in the cloudless sky. Doesn't he share my dance high? Doesn't John get that this whole scenario would entirely seduce just about any girl on the planet?

Apparently not, because when he is satisfied that he has thoroughly worked the left foot, he moves on to the right. I silently sit on top of the bench for thirty minutes, watching the moon above me and John's head below me, feeling his hands on me and thinking how ironic it is that I don't want to be involved with anyone and here is this man who seems to agree with that, and all I can think is, *PLEASE kiss me!*

When John releases my foot and stands up, he looks at

me with a flat, decidedly unamorous expression.

"I'll walk you to your car," he says.

We walk slowly down the quay of the marina toward the parking lot. John carries my shoes and talks softly. We are laughing and comfortable and when we get to my car, he leans against it and continues to talk for a half-hour more. I'm feeling hopeful. I'm feeling like, maybe if I push things along a little. . . .

"Monday is Memorial Day," I say nonchalantly. "My brother and I are taking a bunch of friends out on his boat for the day. Would you like to come?"

John stands up straighter and steps away from the car.

"I don't know what I'm doing Monday. I think we're going scuba diving."

"Well, if you don't go, you're welcome to join us." Suddenly I'm feeling adolescent and shy.

"Okay."

"You can . . . you know, call me at the last minute Monday morning."

"We'll see."

Finally, John awkwardly kisses me on the cheek and I miss it because I'm unprepared and surprised and already moving to get into the car. He shuts the door, gives a quick wave through the window, and walks away.

On Monday Bret and I go up the Intracoastal to Peck Island with a group of friends. We spend the day anchored up, lazing around on the boat, swimming to shore, running through the dunes to the other side of the island where the deep green Atlantic crashes against the pristine, tourist-free beach. That night we go to a poolside barbecue at a friend's house. John never calls.

Just Another Night of Salsa

The following Thursday John and I go for our salsa night at Noche. The place is packed. The summer season is in full swing and while this might be considered the off-season for tourism, it is a busy local season. Businessmen out on the patio wear button-down shirts yanked askew by the ripping off of ties. Women have slipped into their tightest, strappiest dresses with their hair swept up into ponytails and twists. In Florida the same jubilation for summer exists as in the Northeast. Easiness settles into everyone and Noche hums with a sort of happy, pulsating energy. The dance crowd spills into the lounge area, and fog machines work double time trying to cool down an atmosphere overheated in more ways than one.

John leads me to the dance floor. As I slip through the crowd I wave at the Freak, who grins, nods, and winks at me. The three-piece combo fills Noche with steamy Latin music. In the middle of the floor John turns to face me and we easily pick up the beat and begin to dance. It's just another night of salsa as we've had before, but John and I are closer in sync. I'm getting better and better. I don't have to stand and listen to the music for a minute before I find the beat. I turn without getting too far away from him. I keep my steps small. I make sure to stay within a tiny range of the floor, which makes our timing and style much more smooth and consistent. Finally, too, I follow John's embellishments; they no longer throw me off rhythm. I even embellish on my own for a few seconds without feeling lost on the floor.

When we dance the chemistry between us pulses with increasing palpability. We keep our eyes locked on each other's. Our bodies press against each other, melding into a single swaying force, whether the dance requires it or not. We salsa, bachata, and merengue in virtually the same embrace and on a whole other level, like a couple who both know what they're doing. I'm in a heady glow realizing I am, finally, becoming a decent partner. In a lull between songs, a Latin woman approaches us. She sports a wide smile that extends from one to the other of her big-hoop-ear-ringed ears.

"Habla español?"

We shake our heads. The woman thinks for a second and then says very slowly, "You dance very pretty. Si, muy linda." She squeezes my hand and walks off the floor repeating, "Muy linda, muy linda."

At the end of the evening John, drenched in sweat, piggybacks me and my aching feet from Noche to the bench by the Intracoastal where he proceeds, once more, to silently massage each sole. Again, I sit up on the back of the bench looking at John's head below me. In profile, his hair hangs down over his right eye. I reach out with one finger to push the hair back, then trace my fingertip over his head down to his neck. John continues massaging my foot but holds himself very still. He doesn't look at me when again I softly run my finger over his forehead, then up over his hair down to his neck.

I put my hands back in my lap. John finishes one foot and moves on to the other, until I can walk to the car. He leans his back against the driver's door and we talk. Then he reaches out and puts his hands on my hips, a fluid gesture made without any facial recognition or halt to the conversation. I answer the motion with a step toward him, and he slips his arms around my waist. My hands gently rest on his biceps and I lean against his hips. In the middle of chatting, he slowly tilts his head to the side, lowers his face toward me, and moves his lips close to mine. He does not kiss me but hovers there. I stand completely still. I wait as long as I can.

And then I can't wait another second. Just as I start to close the distance between us, John does, too, so that we kiss each other at the same time, both of us simultaneously making that final movement that joins us together.

Oh, what a kiss!

John kisses the way he dances: softly and sensuously, full of passion and romance with the underlying strength of some emotion that remains undivulged. We stand there in the parking lot, kissing, pressed against each other in the warm breeze.

"What took you so long?" I murmur.

"I wanted to be sure you agreed."

Finally John opens the car door and I slide behind the wheel. He leans into the car for one long, final kiss.

I drive home full of relief and anticipation.

Rumba Queen

People say Bill Hering looks like the actor Gary Busey, but he's much more handsome than that. Busey looks old and worn and washed-out. While Bill's features may exhibit certain similarities, he exudes happiness, life, and vitality. He's got a dancer's body today, but in his casual movements you can still see the ghost of a former rock-band drummer and high school football star. Standing almost six feet tall with short, straight blond hair and bright blue eyes, Bill began dancing at the age of nineteen and went on to become a U.S. Silver Medalist before marrying his partner and starting a family.

I've taken a couple of group Latin classes with Bill, who owns the Ritz with his wife. What I love about his teaching style is that Bill can break down any dance by individual beat, bar of music, and/or step. And then show you how to put it all back together again. A phenomenal dancer, Bill puts equal energy into every step and every move of any style and injects it with enough of his personal technique so the dance becomes an expression of his own self. He also happens to be a really good guy. His friendly and kind eyes sparkle with mirth and he has a wicked and quick sense of humor. His face, long and soft-jawed, never seems without a naughty glimmer and a ready smile.

I first met Bill at one of the Ritz ballroom parties when he led me through a fox-trot; even though I wasn't proficient at the dance, I didn't misstep or stumble—I danced, which is why I decide Bill is the perfect Henry Higgins to my dance-challenged Eliza Doolittle. I realize that if I'm going to be seeing John, I have a lot of catching up to do.

"I need you to work with me on styling," I tell Bill the next time I see him in the studio.

Bill stands behind the bar at the back of the studio drinking a Bud Light and twirling a pair of reading glasses. He has the kind of smile that's so genuine you think he must not smile at anyone the way he smiles at you.

"You look great out there."

"Thank you! But John's so accomplished at the Latin and ballroom dances. I need a crash course."

"Then let's get started, kid." Bill tosses the beer bottle in the trash and takes a cinnamon Altoid from the constantly refilled tin on the bar. "How's tomorrow at four?"

he asks, popping the mint in his mouth.

"Perfect. One more thing: Don't tell John I'm studying with you. I want to surprise him."

"Ohhhhh." Bill's eyes twinkle with glee. "I like it!"

I ENTER THE STUDIO for my first private lesson with Bill wholly expecting to have an easy time.

Bill announces, "We'll begin with the rumba."

"The rumba?!" I wrinkle my nose. "I don't really . . . like the rumba. I want to do salsa! And I need to learn waltz."

"Everyone begins with rumba. It contains elements of all the other dances. Once you learn rumba, you can apply those fundamentals to any of the other ballroom dances."

"It's just so . . . *dramatic*."

"That's why it's fun!" Bill demonstrates a couple of steps.

I wrinkle my nose again.

"You don't like the slow and sensual style?"

"That's not really *my* style."

"Why not?"

"It just feels . . . slow. And exposed."

"The key is to use your body to emote. The good thing about rumba is that the music *is* slow. You can learn technique at a very simple pace."

In theory, then, considering the work I did with Flavius, I should be the Rumba Queen by now. People who have no dance background at all—who have never stepped foot on a dance floor—begin with rumba and become proficient in it and I, someone who's been doing some sort of dancing since I began ballet at the age of four, cannot get a grip on it. This is only the beginning of my rumba shame.

"You should always have a metronome going in your head," Bill says. "The count for American Rumba is 1, 2, 3, and 4. Let's see what you've got."

We commence to dance. As awkward as a baby giraffe, I immediately step ahead of the beat.

"Use your arms! Really get into it. Dance like you're the sexiest woman on earth!"

Bill's commands only make me more stiff. He observes my discomfort for a few minutes and then says, "I know what your problem is: You're not a showoff. That's okay. You can be a subtle dancer, but still use your whole body. Relax."

I try to relax. I try to tell my body to do whatever it's supposed to do, but I don't get any reaction from it.

"Shoulders down." Bill says.

Oh, here we go . . .

I step through a turn twice as fast as the music.

"Drag your feet a little along the floor. If you track, you'll naturally slow down."

Bill locks the embrace, so I have no choice but to go at the speed he allows.

"Better. You're just like I was when I started dancing. I had a lot of energy and I had to learn to properly channel and control it." Bill whips me into a spiral turn that I land with a horribly off-balance step.

I break out of the embrace and walk away. "Dance is so humiliating! Just when you think you know what you're doing, you discover you really don't. I know how to do a spiral. I don't know why I didn't just land it."

Bill laughs. "Come back here." We assume the embrace and slowly begin again. "I always used to be questioning myself and my instructors. It's good. It means you're learning."

Bill leads me into a Cuban walk, one of my least favorite moves because it suspends me out to the side of my partner, going around him in a circle, connected only by one hand. I have to float out there forever until he snaps my hand and brings me back in. That open space feels like a sort of no-man's land. It makes me nervous. When Bill doesn't bring me back in quickly, I get panicky. In a fit of desperation I turn myself back to face Bill and close the gap between us.

"Hey," he chides. "Don't you trust me to lead?"

"I was afraid I would miss the lead," I lie.

"You can't be thinking about that. Picture each move as its own individual figure in its own individual moment. Imagine you're just doing the most perfect Cuban walk— that's it. There will never be anything else. Focus on the walk, put everything you've got into the present moment. Let the lead surprise you." He takes a breath, then continues. "You need to develop some trust in yourself, Michele. Pretend you are securely confident. *Be* securely confident. You have to love yourself, Michele, and you have to love the rumba. Love the rumba! *Loooove* the rumba!"

Shifting

I hate the rumba. I really do. I hate everything about this West Indian dance that somehow, in the middle of the Great Depression, became an American standard. I hate the sentimentality of the music. I hate the drama of the dance's expression. I hate the way your free arm always has to be moving up and down (elbows first) or in and out (think ballet). I hate the way you have to hold the fingers of your free hand like you've got a pencil balanced on top of fingers three and four, below two and five. I hate that you're supposed to *emote*. I hate the way you have to settle into one hip at the same time you lift the opposite one. I hate Latin motion and the Cuban walk which, to a born and bred American, feel incredibly foreign and over the top. I hate that the rumba is John's favorite ("because it's the most romantic of all the dances"), which means there's no way I can avoid a serious study of it if I want to please him.

Most of all, I hate that I'm really struggling with this, the most rudimentary of all the Latin dances. I overrotate my hips trying to manufacture the Latin motion that is supposed to naturally occur from bending and straightening the knee. I forget to move my free arm, so it dangles like a paralyzed limb at my side. I rush the beat and step too fast because I'm afraid I'm going to miss the lead for the next move, and also because I just feel plain stupid whenever I try to internalize.

"Own the floor!" Bill tells me. I'm supposed to snap my head on 2 and look sultry and beguiling. When I peek at myself in the mirrors covering the dance studio walls, however, I do not own the floor. I do not look sultry or beguiling. I only look unsure, self-conscious, stiff, and awkward.

As a follower, I must always submit to the lead, which I still find difficult to do. Partner dancing is organized, contained, demanding and full of moments exposing me as good or bad, accomplished or idiotic, graceful or clumsy. It is also challenging and exhilarating, educational, and addicting. Though I can't stop complaining, I am hooked.

"The most important thing in partner dancing," Bill explains in a voice bubbling with a sinus infection that won't go away, "is the connection between the partners. The point is to approach each partner like you're starting a love affair. You must drop your defenses and allow someone to inhabit your space. Like this." Bill takes a big step toward me until his face is only an inch from mine. His chest presses forward; his body elongates and holds itself poised like a stretched rubber band.

I immediately step back. Bill shakes his head with a rueful smile.

"Let's start with the simplest connection," he says. "The hands."

We move into an open embrace, which means my left hand on his right shoulder, his right hand just below my left shoulder blade, and my right hand (arm held at a ninety-degree angle) cupped in the palm of his left. A space of about four to six inches remains between us. Bill pushes his left hand forward; I allow my right arm to go limp and move back.

"Don't collapse your frame," he says, adjusting my right elbow back to ninety degrees. "Your arm should be attached to your spine. This is your frame," he indicates the L of my arm connected to my shoulder. Without stepping forward he presses my hand again. This time, I press back.

"Much better," he says. When I get used to it, allowing Bill to be in control is actually pretty soothing. I allow myself to give in to him a little, which is not exactly comfortable but does, somewhere deep in the recesses of my mind, ignite a very small light like a lantern that sways in the wind at the end of a dark and windy street.

It's a great relief when Bill tells me, "You'll be a better dancer if you don't think." He guides me into a natural underarm turn and, without considering the various angles of the various outcomes, I just go, tilting my head a little under the rotation.

"That's good, that's good," he croons. "See how easy this is? You're doing great."

I try to stop seeking Bill's validation of my every move. I pay attention to his fingers and only react to their cues.

"Close your eyes," he says.

I arch my eyebrows for a moment, regard him, and then do as he requests. We continue moving slowly, forward and back, side to side. Finally we stop and he steps toward me without leading me backward. I open my eyes but don't move away. Bill steps in again. I hold my ground, waiting. Bill moves a little more toward me. I force my body not to instinctively step away. He takes another small step and another until we stand face to face. For a moment we remain utterly still.

"Nice," Bill smiles. "Now we're getting somewhere."

The studio is dark and cool. After each lesson I reemerge into the bright summer heat feeling demoralized by my persisting inadequacies, but also elated. Despite my discomfort, each week I accomplish one small but significant motion. For a fleeting second, I get out of my own way.

Clearly, some attitude is shifting. Something about trying to be a good dancer is unifying my body, heart, and mind. Even if just for a couple of seconds every now and then, I achieve a surprising new degree of harmony. Maybe this result is true of any sport done well. But I've played tennis and softball. I've ridden horses. I've tried golf. Nothing simultaneously engages and satisfies my mind's intellect, my heart's emotion, and my body's desires the way dance does. Nothing else so completely touches and unites all the primal passions buried deep within my soul. I didn't expect this. When I started dancing I only thought I was chasing joy. I didn't expect to find self-unity.

With all of this dance and fun and joy, a sense of calm arises, which opens up a sort of empty space. I feel the anxious urge to fill it, so I start writing again. I sit down to finish the book believing that the new feelings I've been experiencing will make it easier. Still, the material affects me deeply. Over the next two months I descend into that same insane, sleep-deprived depression that always comes when I give myself over to the past. September rolls around and my hair falls out. I'm still dancing four or five nights a week, but even that action isn't powerful enough to stop the avalanche of sadness. Neither is the fact that I am, as it turns out, falling in love with John.

At first it is just an instinct, a quiet impulse to love, and then the feeling gathers itself into John's shape. No rush of overwhelming emotion here, only a wonderful partnership on and off the dance floor with a man who seems the most happy, genuine, romantic, and incredibly good person I have ever met. He also happens to be one of the most emotionally introverted people I've ever met. John feels deeply but does not show it, so there are no discussions about our relationship or our future or how we feel. There are no declarations, only eyes that meet, and smiles, and arms tightly protecting me deep in the night. Which means this all happens at a very good pace for me. When I notice, for example, that I love him, it is in ordinary moments that suddenly seem remarkable.

A tae kwon do third-degree black belt not prone to introspection, John surprises me with his philosophical thoughts. I was upfront with him when we officially began dating. I laid out the PTSD facts and explained that I was struggling.

"I believe in you," he said simply.

Now I always get from him a very simple, clean, and well-examined perspective when I test my thoughts and identity theories on his linear, pragmatic mind.

Recently, I've been trying to figure out what I want my personal philosophy for living to be. I ask John his opinion when we are in bed on a Sunday morning, gradually waking up from a late night at Coco Bongo. John absently strokes

Baylee's belly.

"What's your personal philosophy for living?" I ask, propping myself on an elbow.

The man doesn't even need to think about it.

"There are three parts. First, to enjoy every day. Second, to be kind to others. Third, to be helpful."

"When did you decide all of that?"

He shrugs. "It's just the way I've always been."

But even my growing adoration of John (and the fact that I am greatly benefiting from his life philosophy) does not save me from the cycle of myself. I haven't slept more than three hours a night for the past two weeks. I've lost weight. My hair is, if it's possible, even thinner.

Soon, the year will come to a close. My fortieth birthday looms only a few months away. I am still not free. I hover on the threshold of stepping into and assuming a new self, but an attachment to my old self lingers. Something radical must be done.

Lately, I've been hearing a radio commercial advertising hypnosis as a cure for nicotine addiction. I decide to place the momentum in someone else's alternative expertise. If hypnosis can break the body's cravings for an addiction, perhaps it can break the mind's cravings, too.

Retraining My Brain

I approach the task of finding a hypnotherapist halfheartedly because I don't really believe in hypnotism. I gather names because I am desperate, not because the idea inspires faith. I have in my mind a memory of a hypnosis session in the fall of 1986. My freshman year of college I took the ubiquitous Psychology 101 class with about 150 other students. Halfway through the semester, the professor and his teaching assistants asked for volunteers for a hypnosis research project. The point of the study was to see how easily hypnotizable random subjects were. We were told not to try to give in to hypnosis, but just to allow it to happen naturally. I was, by the age of eighteen, already incredibly hyperaroused and hypervigilant. I went into the project knowing I would be The One Who Would Not Give In. The hypnosis session lasted about twenty minutes. I felt smug when the TA gave up.

Now, I compile a list of hypnotherapists nearby and systematically begin making phone calls. I discover I immediately like this holistic health group: They advocate speaking with you before you even make an appointment. You could never call an internist and say, *I'd like a few moments before I commit,* but hypnotherapists welcome that chance to connect. What's more, they'll spend over thirty minutes doing it.

I have a list of questions I put to each one. The first, *Can you cure Post-Traumatic Stress Disorder?,* gets the same reply from everyone, *Yes.* Right off the bat I see I'm going to have to revise my technique. I begin asking each therapist to outline his or her background, qualifications, and some personal examples of PTSD results. I weed out the woman who says her success is due to her devotion to the Unitarian Church. I quickly end the call with the woman who is so hyper and frazzled I don't think I could relax anywhere in her vicinity. I cross off the name of the man who will chat with me about himself and hypnotherapy, but evades answering any of my specific questions.

I narrow down the field to two and spend a long time on the phone with each. One is a male in his sixties; the other a female in her fifties. One heads a large PTSD healing center; one directs a hypnotherapy center. The man says he'll cure me in one day for $1,500, no matter how long it takes. It could take two hours, he says, or it could take nine.

"We'll just keep working until we've resolved all of your issues," he says. But I'm afraid that, as I did with Greg, every time we uncover one issue we'll uncover a whole host more and the day with this guy will never end. Also, I can't imagine, no matter how good this guy might be, that we can cure twenty-five years of issues in one single day.

The woman, on the other hand, says we'll need to take it one $125-an-hour-session at a time. Laura explains, "The practice of hypnosis dates all the way back to Egypt in 3,000 BC. It works from the assumption that the subconscious mind is the storage space of all our past experiences and emotions. In this incredibly vast warehouse, traumatic events are filed in neural pathways that stimulate both physical and emotional reactions that can affect the immune system and overall health. Hypnosis transforms the subconscious mind and reprograms the neural pathways through a process of suggesting new perceptions and beliefs in response to old experiences.

"The truth is," she continues, "we all go in and out of trance states all the time. Have you ever driven down the highway and missed your exit because you just weren't paying attention?"

"Sure."

"That's because you were in a trance state! Have you ever been reading and lost track of time?"

"Yes."

"That's because you were in hypnosis. Hypnosis is only an altered state of focus. When you watch TV or the movies or do anything during which you don't feel the actual passage of time that's hypnosis. It's a natural process the brain likes and understands. You will be aware of your surroundings and can always choose to come out of hypnosis at any time. You will remain totally in control in every moment while choosing to relax to such a degree that the conscious mind will let down its defenses so we can get some work done."

All this sounds reasonable, but still I'm skeptical.

Finally, Laura shares some of her own story with me. In a chirpy southern drawl she explains how she, too, had a severe trauma she needed to overcome and how she did it through hypnotherapy. I realize this convenient example could be part of her sales pitch, but she's the only hypnotherapist I've spoken to who has related her own deep belief in the success of this bizarre process. I choose her.

I breeze into Laura's office acting happy and cheerful and nonchalant. In other words: a complete fake. I chat and laugh and joke around and do everything I can to hide the pain I'm in because I want Laura to like me. I want her to enjoy helping me. I want to be not a pitiful patient but just some woman seeking a better balance in her life. A few inches over five feet, Laura has a cap of close-cropped wavy gray hair and warm, soft brown eyes. She's got a perfect ski slope nose and a generous mouth. She wears no makeup. Her warm, smiling, kind, and utterly genuine expression makes faking it seem an insult.

I curl up on the couch in her office and tuck my feet beneath my legs. Laura sits with perfect posture opposite me on a small swivel chair. She dons a pair of ruby red reading glasses and picks up a pen and clipboard.

"Tell me everything," she says.

As I tell her the condensed version of 1981 to the present, Laura writes all over the pad, every which way. Sometimes, she doesn't even look at the paper; she keeps her eyes on me with unwavering attention and writes and writes and writes. It doesn't take long for me to drop my guard. By the end of the tale, I am in a tearful puddle of self-pity and desolation.

When the final sentence ends, Laura deliberately looks at me and says, as if making a promise, "I'm going to help you with this."

A physical wave of relief washes over me. No health care professional has ever said those words to me.

"We are going to get rid of this trauma once and for all," Laura continues. "I guarantee it. Hypnosis saved me from suicide, so I know it works. But first, there are some things I need to tell you." She pauses to adjust the height of her seat and then leans toward me.

"The first thing I have to tell you, and the most important thing for you to understand, is that 88 percent of your brain is your subconscious; 12 percent is your rational mind. The 12 percent that functions logically makes you feel like you're in control, but it's the 88 percent—where you feel—that's really guiding and informing everything you do. That 88 percent is who you really are. The other 12 percent is merely a construct designed to get you through the day-to-day.

"When a trauma occurs, the magnitude of the experience is absorbed into your subconscious. It's like a hand leaving an imprint in the sand: even when the hand is removed, the sand retains the shape. The actual experience of the hand in the sand no longer exists, but the sand continues to behave as if it does. Trauma and the subconscious are like this. The 88 percent holds the imprint long after an experience ends. The job of the subconscious, actually, is to keep you safe. After trauma your subconscious takes that job very seriously. It will do anything—even adopt negative behaviors—in order to keep you safe; sometimes it can be a little too earnest and excitable. When these protective measures no longer serve you, that's when you feel the need to change. Change, however, is difficult to bring about because the subconscious mind is devoted to its imprinted perceptions. Through suggestions made directly to the subconscious mind, hypnotherapy changes perceptions of memories, which in turn helps change perceptions of the self and ultimately, behavior."

Cool, I'm thinking. *Sounds like I won't have to work so hard.*

Laura continues. "The subconscious mind stores the memory of not only everything you experience, but also everything you think, feel, fantasize, and dream about, day or night. The reason for this is that your subconscious mind cannot tell the difference between something that's actually happening and something you are imagining. The subconscious records everything equally and responds to both the real and the imagined with the same intensity, both during an event and also afterward. Hypnosis uses this concept to help you reprogram your behavior by using the imagination to help you change what your subconscious thinks and feels. Are you with me so far?"

I nod.

"While we cannot change memories, we can update how we feel about them. We can retrain your brain. In order to do this, the critical factor of the conscious mind must be bypassed so the subconscious mind can be accessed. The role of hypnosis, then, is to revise, relieve, or erase those impressions that are not serving you. When you do the same thing in the same way with enough repetition, the subconscious mind makes it a habit. A habit is an automatic response to a certain situation in a specific way. You don't think, you just react—97 percent of what you do every day is by habit. When you get up and get dressed in the morning, that's a habit. You don't think about it, you just automatically do it. Our subconscious develops habit patterns that either help or hurt us. Luckily, habits can be changed."

I think of all the PTSD keep-me-safe habits I have. Am I ready to release them? For a second I feel ambivalent about letting go, and then I remember that partially it's those habits that brought me to Laura in the first place.

"Our job here is to change your attitude toward those perceptions and beliefs that are causing you pain," Laura says. "You've already outlined several of them in the thirty minutes you've been here. The goal of hypnosis is to change behavior. One of the ways we do this is through direct suggestion. All you will need to do is relax your mind. Reaching the subconscious requires no effort, no concentration. It's simply a matter of allowing, not forcing. When you allow yourself to relax, you're in the most receptive state of consciousness."

I want to stop Laura and explain that my mind doesn't know how to relax. It's always running with anxiety, fear, and planning. I stop myself from speaking out by focusing on what made me choose to work with her. I feel comfortable with her. I believe in who Laura is, what she knows, what she's done, and what she thinks we can do. I have nothing else to go on except hope.

"The next thing I need you to understand is this: Imagination is as strong as knowledge. What we're going to do in here will engage your creative mind." Laura moves to the edge of her seat. "The suggestions I give in hypnosis will stimulate your imagination so that it uses its power to reinform your subconscious mind about the beliefs you hold.

Beliefs such as," and here Laura refers to her notes. She reads back my statements in direct quotes. "'I can't let it go.' 'I don't feel safe.' 'I'm so afraid.' 'I feel powerless.' 'There's always something wrong with me.' We're going to change all of those thoughts by engaging your imagination. We'll reframe your ideas and beliefs so they are more positive and harmonious for your well-being. It's important to know that in the same way the imagination can help you reach your goals, it can prevent you from reaching them, too. Many of the difficulties you experience in your life probably originate in your imagination; beliefs are so powerful, your mind transforms them into reality. The 88 percent overrides the 12 percent."

Laura takes a sip of water and continues.

"Finally, you have stressful thought patterns that have been going on for years. In hypnosis the suggestions will be geared toward rewriting these patterns and forming new ones that will bring you a feeling of peace and safety. It's not only your subconscious mind we'll be tapping here. Your conscious mind will need to participate, too. All the hypnotherapy in the world won't work if you don't want it to. You must actively want to engage in this process. Also, you need to carefully monitor your thoughts. If you fill your subconscious with negative thoughts, feelings, and images, you will soon begin to experience all of those things. What you put your energy on is what is created. Any time you have a negative thought—for example, any time you think, 'I am powerless'—I want you to say to yourself, 'Cancel.' As in, 'Cancel that negative thought.' For myself, I use the image of a purple elephant. It is so ridiculous and out of the ordinary, it immediately takes my mind off whatever negative thought I'm having."

Laura's eyes get big and excited. "You must allow and reinforce only positive thoughts. Cancel negative statements and replace them with the opposite. For example: 'I am powerless' becomes 'I am powerful.' Will you be able to do this?"

I nod, "Yes."

"Good, then you won't be working against yourself. The mental attitude you hold when you hear a suggestion determines whether it is accepted into your subconscious mind for change or flat out rejected. There are three mental attitudes that affect the hypnotic state. The first is one of complete embrace; you passionately want and trust the suggestion. Because of this, the suggestion goes into your subconscious and change occurs. The other two attitudes—if you're uncomfortable with the suggestion or if you don't care about it at all—will cause you to reject the suggestion and no change will occur. You have to really want the suggestions to come to life, so it's important that you whole-heartedly embrace them. Any questions?"

I'm trying to take in all this information, and only shake my head.

"One final thing: Hypnotherapy is not like talk therapy. In here we will not focus on the past. There's no need to do that. We don't need to keep going over and over what happened. Going back isn't what heals us; going forward does. With hypnotherapy we focus on the future so you can see what you're walking toward rather than constantly looking back at what you're running from. By activating your subconscious, we're going to create and liberate the new you from the authentic self submerged beneath all this other stuff."

Laura's energetic attitude transforms everything into something simple and manageable. All this time I've felt controlled by the past, but Laura's outlook makes it seem that she and I control a future where the past is inconsequential. I'm fervently wishing this hour would never end. I wish I had looked into hypnotherapy years ago.

Finally satisfied she's given me enough of a foundation, Laura suggests I move to the recliner. She turns off the overhead light, switches on a small lamp, and pulls her swivel chair beside me. I lean back in the seat and take a deep, relaxing breath.

In a different voice, low and throaty, Laura says, "Close your eyes and listen to the sound of my voice. Move your body into a comfortable position and . . . *relax*. In a moment I'm going to tell you to open your eyes, and then close your eyes. This will be a sign to your body to let go and relax. Okay. Now: Open your eyes. And close your eyes. Feel your body letting go. Release all tension from your muscles. Feel your toes relax. And your ankles relax. Your shins relax. And your knees relax."

Slowly Laura relaxes everything up through my scalp to the top of my head before she counts backward from 100 to 93 and then . . .

"I want you to picture a room with an open roof. Place two chairs in the room. Sit down in one of the chairs. In the chair facing you, place a repository box that has a red helium balloon attached to it. In the box I want you to put, one by one, all of your fear related to your illness, all of your anger, all of your sadness, all of your negative and disturbing emotions relating to 1981 and any health problems you've had since then. Put your pain in the box. Put your terror in the box. Put anxiety in the box. Put suffering in the box. Put all of those feelings you've had over the years in relation to your trauma into the box. When the box is full, close it and then let it lift up through the open roof and watch it float away.

"Now, see you in the chair opposite. You are facing yourself and I want you to look at you and forgive yourself for all the negative emotions you have felt about your illness. Forgive yourself for the pain and terror and fear. Forgive yourself for the sadness and illness and all other sicknesses. Forgive yourself for not being able to find a way to let it go. And I want you to tell yourself that it is okay to forgive anyone and everyone who has ever participated in causing these negative things that you have felt. Forgive your mother and your father. Forgive the doctors and the nurses. Forgive everyone who has knowingly or unwittingly contributed to your suffering. Forgive yourself. Now, hug yourself real tight, and then let yourself shrink down to an inch and land in your heart." When Laura says the word heart, she touches two of her fingertips to my upper arm.

This whole time my eyes are closed and I am lying back in the recliner. I am disappointingly awake. While I did not expect to be asleep, I thought I would be at least in some state of altered consciousness. Instead, my mind's critical factor seems hard at work. With every new image I work hard to create in my mind, the whole time I'm thinking this all seems like a childish and ridiculous exercise. My conscious mind is not at all fooled. This is all very nice, but I am still fully alert. In fact, I'm so critically aware that I'm thinking this is all some hoax. What happened to all that stuff about setting aside the conscious mind? Instead, my mind is still its usual busy self, coding and decoding all the information every second. It's still alert enough to conclude: This is not working! Shrink down to an inch? Put emotions in a box? *Come on, lady,* I want to say, *bring on the good stuff!* And then it dawns on me that maybe this is the good stuff and the problem is that I really am, as the TA decided all those years ago, unhypnotizable.

Laura continues to guide me from one visualization to another. Between each instruction she advises me to "go deeper, and deeper, *relaxed.*" She chants for a little while "attitude of gratitude, attitude of gratitude" and touches my arm. I find myself wondering what that's supposed to mean. I'm on the verge of opening my eyes and saying, "Hey, we didn't discuss this attitude of gratitude. What's it about?" But I keep my eyes and mouth shut. This is all turning out to be a lot like the guided meditations we had in the playwriting course I once took where we lay all over the floor of a room, eyes closed, body relaxed, and invented characters based on the guided visualizations provided by the instructor. I'm disappointed, but I let Laura do her thing.

Eventually she says, "In a moment I'm going to count to three. When I reach the number three, and not before, you will open your eyes and feel awake and alert and wonderful in every way. One. Feel the energy return to your body, moving up from the soles of your feet. Two. Your eyes feel as if they're being bathed beneath the water of a cool mountain stream. Get ready now. Three. Open your eyes. Feel your body refill with a wonderful energy. You are awake and alert and feeling wonderful and marvelous in every way."

Since I've been so conscious the whole time, I'm surprised, as I open my eyes, to feel as if I'm waking from a nap. My eyelids are heavy and I feel a little disoriented in the room. I feel the urge to stretch. I look at Laura. She smiles.

"That was very good," she says, patting my hand.

"It was?"

"We did some good work."

"I thought I'd feel something . . . "

"How do you feel?"

I shrug. "A little groggy."

"How long do you think that hypnosis session lasted?"

I check my infallible internal clock. "About fifteen minutes, maybe less."

Laura's smile gets wider. "It was almost forty minutes. In hypnosis your usual critical faculties don't function normally. Your sense of time, for example, is distorted."

Laura has turned on the overhead light now, and I am pretty sure I feel exactly the same as when I walked in here.

Laura, though, seems pleased. As she walks me out of the building, she is full of cheery support and encouragement.

"Stop writing that book!" she says. "Let yourself be. We have more important things to do."

Weird State of Bliss

I complain to John that night, "Hypnosis is a waste of time."

"Let's just wait and see," he advises.

I crawl into bed with the usual resignation. I accept the nightmare will come, hypnosis or not; I only hope I'll be able to fall back to sleep afterward. But I sleep deeply and undisturbed for eight hours straight and awaken the next morning feeling completely rested, as if I've just slept for a century. This continues for five nights. On the sixth morning I wake with an extreme feeling of profound mental and physical peace. I feel incredibly safe and secure. I don't immediately begin scanning my environment, as usual, for what could go wrong, will go wrong, has gone wrong. I don't immediately survey possible dangers, or bolt shut the door to the past because something keeps pressuring the hinges, threatening to push through.

I feel void of tension and anxiety. I feel . . . *good*. And also optimistic in a vague, nonspecific way. Here I am after a single hypnotherapy session and suddenly all of that junk is gone. I do not feel afraid. I do not feel the need to test myself. I do not feel driven to produce something of meaning. The day begins; I am awake. That is production enough. I have the sense everything is okay. More than that: it is okay for me to be okay. I'm so peaceful I spend the day walking around in a weird state of bliss. Do people everywhere feel this way? It's occurring to me that my perceptions of what is normal are horribly off.

Each morning I get out of bed slowly and go through my strength-training routine waiting for the familiar rush of tension, but it doesn't arrive. Instead, I spend the day in a state of suspended calm that continues into the following day and the day following that, until all of this incredible calmness begins to really freak me out. I feel like I've forgotten something very important and I'm going to remember it too late. I call Laura.

"I'm sorry to bother you, but I'm feeling very strange."

"Define strange."

"This is going to sound crazy, but I'm feeling very— in my body, I mean, in my limbs—at peace. I feel more present in myself. I feel more comfortable in my own skin. As if I am who I should be. As if I'm doing exactly what I should be doing. As if I don't have a past that matters."

"And this is bad?"

"Well, I've never felt this kind of serenity before."

"That's not strange, that's good!"

"But I never feel at peace. I never feel as if everything's all right. And now, somewhere deep inside, this unfamiliar sensation of peace is radiating."

"That was the goal."

"I know, but all of this tranquility . . . it's making me nervous!"

Laura laughs.

"How long will this feeling last?" I need to know.

"It's permanent!"

"I'm afraid it's going to go away. I don't want to get too used to it."

"Michele, everything you're saying is completely normal. Hypnosis causes some immediate and some slower changes. We're restructuring the 88 percent of your brain. You are going to begin noticing alterations in your behavior and your attitudes, in your beliefs and actions. Everything is all right! You should feel at peace! How are the nightmares?"

"I haven't had a single one since I saw you."

"Then relax and enjoy this new state of being! Get used to it; this is the new you."

I tread carefully in my new self. I don't trust it. I wait for it to abandon me at any moment. I am suspicious and disbelieving. I don't imagine you can be one person for twenty-five years and become another overnight. But it hasn't been overnight. I've been trying to make this change for a very, very long time.

While I feel completely different, I am not unfamiliar to myself. A quick rundown of my likes and dislikes reveals no stark changes. A quick overview of my hopes and fears reveals they are all intact, although some of those fears have changed. I am still afraid of what the next medical mistake will be, for example, but now it is a hypothetical fear. Am I the same person I always was, only after 1981 I was carrying a lot of baggage and today I've relinquished some of it? All these years have I been the same self, only hidden under trauma's mask?

My mother and I walk Baylee around the lake by my

house one night. I try to explain all of this to her. She echoes Laura's words.

"You've worked hard, Michele. Just enjoy the results. Turn off your meter and rest."

My mother listens to my theories, commiserates with my struggle, and sometimes just holds me while I sob. It feels good to be close to her again, to not be arguing and pushing her away. When I need to hash out an idea, for example, Mom cooks up dinner and then, on the patio overlooking the golf course behind their home, Mom and Dad and I sit in the evening air and pool our thoughts.

I see Laura again in two weeks. We continue reprogramming the subconscious to stop protecting me and instead allow me to live wholly and fully, believing I am healthy both physically and mentally. I begin to feel strange rushes of emotion. I am on the beach or driving or cooking and then all of a sudden, I feel a surge of what I can only describe as happiness times ten, accompanied by a chaser of gratefulness for this new life I've carved out: for my house, my family, dance, John; for my own determination to put an end to my suffering. In the past I was often on the verge of spontaneous tears. Now I'm on the verge of skipping and singing a psalm of praise for the sun, the beach, Baylee, Laura. It's ridiculous and over the top, but I can't help myself. I feel as if my life since 1981 was in black and white and now suddenly I see everything in Technicolor. Is this who I am when the 88 percent is released from trauma's imprint?

Two months pass. By mid-December I have seen Laura six times. The effects of her work deepen each week. I begin trusting that these new feelings are here to stay. I become accustomed to them, and the initial euphoria eases into a sense of normalcy. After this settling of calm, I begin shedding, not exactly the past, but bits and pieces of armor

I donned to protect myself from it. I envision myself starting over, unifying the essence of who I was Before with who I became After with who I choose to be Now. The years of therapy, research, writing, reconstructing identity, dance, hypnosis—all of it finally seems to be coalescing into some ultimate transformation that will allow me to live without trauma's effects.

The war is ending. I feel my survivor self beginning to back down. I sense her retreat into the shadows. She is at peace. She will remain with me, but she has relinquished control to another self who desires to feel and experience and create joy.

I Am a Dancer

The weekend before Christmas, John packs for a trip out West. Each year he and his mother travel to Washington State to visit his siblings for the holidays. Tonight will be our last Saturday together until after the new year. We are going to La Fonda, a delicious Cuban restaurant in West Palm Beach. After 10 p.m. it turns from eatery into nightclub, and a DJ spins a terrific mix of salsa, bachata, merengue, cumbia, vallenato, and tropicale.

The entire staff and all patrons are Latin. We are the only gringos, but every Saturday night we come to dance and are greeted with hugs and family-like hellos. Prints by Fernando Botero, a Colombian painter, decorate the walls of the club. While darkened booths line the perimeter of the room, several high-top tables surround the dance floor. The age of the crowd ranges from early twenties through sixties and they blend together well.

We arrive early for dinner and order Cuban-style grilled pork and fish with buttered rice, tostones, sweet plantains, and flan for dessert. By the time the DJ sets up, the diners have gone and the clubgoers have yet to arrive, so John and I have the dance floor to ourselves. The DJ spins salsa and while we dance, the club owner, bartenders, waiters, and barbacks sit around the room and watch. They tell us we dance as if we come from the Dominican Republic or Puerto Rico or Peru. My little snake of joy swells up with pride.

The crowd filters in between 11 and midnight. John and I dance almost every song, sitting out only once or twice to catch our breath. We have just returned to the floor when a song begins, a salsa unlike any I've ever heard. The music has a full, rhapsodic sound, bolstered by a melodic passion that reminds me of the anticipation of a much-wanted kiss, that deep-belly desire and squirmy yearning. I immediately feel a surge of happiness and the need to dance. The song is "Te Mando Flores," by Fonseca. *Te mando flores que recojo en el camino,* he croons: "I am sending you flowers which I picked up on the road." *Yo te las mando entre mis suenos*: "I am sending them to you between my dreams." Fonseca croons Spanish words I don't fully understand, but I feel his longing and it makes me dance in a wholly different way.

I am what Bill would call *emoting,* my body rising and falling and moving in response to the poignant elements of the music. I do not just move through the basic salsa step as dancer separate from music. We two meld into one; I dance as a conduit for each individual note. The power of the song surges through me, and my body joyously lifts to meet it. I feel strong and in control. My dancing becomes fluid and creative, a reflection of the transformative power of joy unleashed and set free.

John's having the same response to the song. He looks at me with intense passion and leads me all over the floor with a dominant gentleness. Something about the beat and the rhythm and Fonseca's voice transport us both to another level of connection and ability. We dance as if we share one body and one mind. We execute difficult moves in a rhythm of palpable romance. John's choreography, always a blend of many dances, tonight perfectly weaves into the salsa several elements of Argentine tango that deepen and elaborate the sensuality of the dance. We dance for each other, looking into each other's eyes and merging into one fantastic flow of body, rhythm, movement, and synchronization, creating the most flawless and intricate, sexy and flirtatious, emotional dance we've ever done.

It is not until the song ends and I take my eyes from John that I realize all the other dancers have moved to the sidelines to watch. Those not dancing have turned from their conversations to get a better view. They sit motionlessly or twist around in their chairs and stare. I feel too exhilarated to be embarrassed. The room erupts into applause. I look around and in every direction, along every wall, in every seat, faces smile and hands clap. I look away in shyness at first, then look back at the crowd. A huge smile stretches itself on my face. The moment suspends and I realize that after all the months of lessons and practice and humiliation and struggle and desire, I am finally a dancer. I have found my *sanuk*.

Joy has given me back my strength. That strength is finally setting me free. I wrap my arms around John and give him an enormous kiss.

THIS YEAR I CELEBRATE New Year's Eve twice. John is

out of town, so on December 30th my tango friends and I drive toward Miami to attend a Gala Milonga—a fancy Argentine tango dance party. Dancers from all over the world arrive. A floor show follows a three-course dinner. Dressed in our New Year's best, we dance, rotating from stranger to stranger throughout the evening. I sample the crowd and am excited to find I am proficient in following other leaders besides John.

On New Year's Eve, my parents, Bret, and I go to the Breakers again. Unlike last year, I do not feel like crying. Instead, when Bret and I get on the floor, the band is playing the same covers of popular American songs, but I hear a rumba, or a cha-cha, or a merengue. Bret and I freestyle for a while before he looks at me and says, "Freestyling must be really boring for you now."

I grin sheepishly.

"What dance would you do to this music?"

"Triple-step swing."

Bret holds up his arms and says, "Teach me."

Since Bret has a great sense of rhythm and is comfortable dancing, it doesn't take long for him to follow the basic triple-step swing pattern. When he realizes how simple it is and how well he's following me, his eyes light up with glee.

"Hey, this is fun!" He leads me into an underarm turn.

For the rest of the night, Bret eggs me on to teach him whatever style of dance goes with the music. I teach him the basics of hustle, cha-cha, and rumba. When we switch partners and I dance with my father, I see Bret teaching my mother to swing.

"What are they doing over there?" my father asks.

"Triple-step swing."

"Can you teach me that?"

By the end of the evening the entire family is triple-step

swinging to anything the band plays. Watching my family learn to dance, I feel the impulse to throw my arms around each of them and say, *Thank you! I know it hasn't been easy.* We dance until the band quits and breakfast is served in a mammoth buffet. The four of us sit on the patio balancing plates, looking out at the moon riding the waves on the Atlantic Ocean.

I keep my gratitude to myself. For a little while, I want it to be my own secret that the pain has finally passed. My own secret, too, that it is gone forever.

Answering The Question

I don't like to celebrate my birthday. It has always marked just one more year of my utter disorientation. A quiet dinner with family is usually all I want to do. But this year is different. This February I want to live it up. I'm turning forty and I did, in fact, achieve my New Year's resolution. Since these are both causes for major celebration I decide, as I did New Year's Eve, to celebrate twice.

First, I invite my parents, Bret, John, and seven friends for dinner at my favorite Italian bistro on my birthday itself. I reserve a private room at the back of the restaurant. My mother decorates the table with small votive candles, flowers, and balloons. She hooks up a stereo and VCR. Soft music plays while on a large flat-panel screen, silent home movies of my fourth birthday loop.

John arrives a little early and while my mother arranges details with the hostess, he and I dance alone in the room. Bret has volunteered to video record the evening. He begins with this pre-party dance and then moves on to film guests arriving. We order bottles of wine and tapas. We dig into bruschetta and olives. The room reverberates with the sound of merriment. After the main courses have been ordered, my father stands up and asks for silence. He proposes a toast.

"I'd like to say a few words about Michele," he says. "I'm going to tell you a few things you don't know about her because Michele rarely talks about herself. She's done some interesting things over the past forty years. I'd like to tell you about them because I'm sure she hasn't."

My father proceeds to extol the highlights of my accomplishments and achievements from high school to present day. What my father doesn't know is that none of the events he lists seemed that interesting. At the time of each experience I was in such a fog that I never saw or appreciated it for what it was. They were things to do to push away the past. Listening to him outline the past couple of decades, a portrait slowly emerges. Like those invisible paintings we had as children that slowly appear beneath watery brushstrokes, a whole picture of me reveals something I have not seen: While my narrow perspective has been trauma-oriented, another part of me continued to strive for some semblance of normality. I may have felt lost, but all along some other self bravely struggled toward definition.

My father ends his toast with a special address to me. "Michele, it has been one of the great joys of my life to watch you in everything you do. If the first forty years are any indication, the next 140 are sure to be a hell of a ride. I look forward to sharing it with you. Happy birthday!"

Everyone at the table claps, and I hug my dad. Dinner is served, presents are opened, and a many-candled birthday cake is placed before me. I make a wish and blow out the flames.

"And that wish included all of you!" I tell my assembled family and friends. "Because each of you was invited tonight because you represent some aspect of joy in my life. You are my Joy Luck Club. I want to thank you for sharing this past year with me, and for sharing the years to come. Happy birthday to me!"

It is a weeknight and it is late, but after cake and coffee no one wants to leave. It's almost midnight before we reluctantly retire, reminding ourselves the celebration will continue on Saturday with my second party—it's a double birthday celebration for me and my tango friend Ben, and we have rented a dance studio. I have had a bad cold all week and been partying anyway. By the time Saturday night rolls around I have completely lost my voice, which turns out to be irrelevant. There is no time to talk. Over 100 dancers show up and we are all on the floor all night. Mom and Dad and Bret dance. So does the regular dance crowd, plus my beach friends and Ben's clients and the stragglers who come in because they hear the music from outside. The floor is full of seasoned dancers, as well as people who have never danced before.

After two hours on the floor, John and I take a break. I sit on his lap at one of the cabaret tables with my parents and Bret and some friends. I look around the table at their joyous, animated faces and realize: I have caused this. My idea for a birthday *milonga* has brought this pure delight to those I love. I, the sad, depressed, traumatized zombie of the past twenty-six years, have created an evening full of dance and fun and music and love. And so, this quest for joy has not only helped me heal but enabled me to lift everyone out of the usual and join us all together in an unusual, harmonious, and joyful place. As I was in the raft on the Truckee River, I am back in the bubble a happy family can make and now,

I've expanded it to include more people.

I look at John. He winks, pulls me tightly against his chest, and kisses my neck. I shift my gaze toward the dance floor, where every face shines with a genuine, deeply felt smile. *This is my life,* I think. *This is who I am.* Finally, I can answer Greg's question. I can describe myself as if TENS never happened: I am a dancer. I am a writer, a creator, a lover, a partner, a daughter, a sister, a friend. I am a dog owner, a Floridian, a beachwalker, a homeowner. I am a joy seeker. I am a believer in my self.

I have conquered the past. Now, I am creating my future as a woman who is connected, strong and free.

Epilogue

Every day Baylee and I walk four miles on the beach. I throw a ball while I stroll; Baylee races ahead, pounces on it, and runs into the ocean, where he holds his head up against the oncoming waves. When it is almost time to end our walk, Baylee sits down, faces the horizon, and contemplates the view. I sit beside him on the warm sand, watch the sun play on the water and feel so grateful that I have landed here, at peace in this beautiful place.

I could not have known that January night at Noche when I so innocently decided I wanted to learn to hustle that it was an evening that would change my life. I didn't suspect that learning to dance would allow me to access such a deep well of joy that I would become filled with the courage I needed to recover, or that I would find hypnosis and then reset the course of my life. In the darkness existing in my mind around that time, I wouldn't have believed anyone who told me the process of seeking joy could so naturally lead to healing a personality that had been so badly misshapen. But, in fact, deciding to shift my focus from the horror of the past to the pursuit of joy in the present was the action that finally led me up that staircase and opened the door in my mind. I believe this process of eliciting the state we desire—and then drawing courage and strength from that state—is an incredible tool in making the shift from powerless to powerful. I believe it's a tool any survivor can utilize, whether your desired state is joy, peace, transcendence, etc.

For almost thirty years I obsessed over the minute details of my hospitalization. Through the repetition of memory I catalogued and deconstructed seconds and milliseconds. I tried to find answers to the relentless questions in my mind. I did my best to function within the realm of fear and many disconnected selves, without a clear sense of my direction, and with only a vague idea of what I was attempting to outrun. While I may have felt lost I can see now that all along some other self bravely struggled toward definition.

I have come to believe that a pure, untraumatized, authentic self exists despite our experiences; it is the part that wishes to be whole and free. Within this self, I believe, exists each individual's enormous healing potential.

So much depends, wrote William Carlos Williams, *upon//a red wheel/barrow//glazed with rain/water//beside the white/chickens.* So much depends upon the arranged minutiae of chance, and how we perceive happenstance. *So much depends upon* how we frame experience and allow it to impact the evolution of who we are. *So much depends upon* something beyond psychological strength; something less rational than therapy and more irrational than trust.

So much depends upon faith in our own identity doing its dance with fate.

I no longer suffer nightmares, flashbacks or insomnia. I am not hypervigilant or hyperaroused. Moments of the past no longer invade my present, nor do I live consumed by fearful anxiety. I have been in triggering situations and remained completely calm, collected and able to think and act appropriately. All of my physical issues, symptoms and undiagnosable maladies have completely, spontaneously healed. I no longer avoid my memories or things that remind me of my trauma. I no longer feel, imagine, experience, or behave in any moment as if the past is about to repeat itself in the present. I no longer worry that I will not and cannot live up to what my horrific illness demanded of me, nor am I terrified by what I learned: that we possess a transcendent power—that we are sometimes godly and godlike even insomuch as we are human and earthbound. That we are powerful in those moments we feel powerless, and that in moments of trauma, some part of ourselves taps this source of power and then, even when we think we are powerless and cannot survive, we are stunned to find we do—and even more so to find we have a deep desire to live.

At the end of my recovery journey, I believe it all comes down to this: My life is about who I am in any given moment. It is about feeling my own heartbeat and the emotions held in each thump of my pulse and letting that define who and what I believe myself to be that day. I can't get back to who I was before the world intruded, but I don't need to. While healing is not as simple as turning your gaze it begins with a willingness to do so. It begins with a willingness to imagine some other self. I also believe it begins with our own actions of defiance against the prison of the past and ends by constructing an identity that belongs purely to the present. For every survivor, the multifaceted healing process is the result of an accumulation of many different tools and efforts—for me, that included psychotherapy, several alternative treatment modalities, research, writing, dancing, and hypnosis. Others may find a different route that proves successful.

Reaching this state of freedom reawakened in me the desire to help others not suffer. The answer to that also led me to do something that has made my survival incredibly worthwhile. My first act was to create www.healmyptsd.com, a website devoted to PTSD support, education and information for survivors, caregivers and healing professionals. Secondly, since my recovery I have become certified in hypnosis and Neuro-Linguistic Programming. I've also become a Certified Professional Coach. Now, I work with survivors to help progress their post-trauma recovery. Using the tools that were so tremendous in my own healing, I have the privilege of walking beside others on their journey toward freedom.

From my own experience, professional training, stories I've heard from many survivors, plus my work with clients I am convinced we all have the potential to construct and deconstruct and change ourselves, our brains, and our traumatic connections. Indeed, recent research about neuroplasticity proves more and more of the brain's inherent capacity to heal. The implications of this are an enormous reversal in the idea that the changes PTSD causes cannot be undone. Often, they can. There is hope for us all.

I never found any meaning in what happened to me in September 1981, but I did learn to make meaning come out of it. With the help of the knowledge and expertise of many other voices, I released myself from the past by finally taking action in the present. If I was rendered powerless back then, I have reclaimed my power now.

The trauma expert Judith Lewis Herman writes, "The survivor may wonder how she can possibly give her due respect to the horror she has endured if she no longer devotes her life to remembrance and warning."

I don't wonder anymore. I gave my respect long enough. Now I'd rather dance.

Acknowledgements

I set out to write this book as I'd learned to do everything: alone, isolated and in a great deal of pain and shrouded secrecy. What I've learned through the process, however, is that it's much less painful (and a whole lot easier) to actually birth a book if you build a team of people who offer support, encouragement, feedback and creativity. I've been extremely lucky to have such a team.

Thanks must first be given to my family who, despite how difficult it may have been, never gave up on me. The full importance of their presence defies language. To my mother, even if I don't say a word you know how much your love, patience, guidance, loyalty and above all, belief in me, constantly provided contact and connection in a world where I felt such an extreme dearth of both. To my father, who has become my business mentor, thank you for sustaining in me the entrepreneurial spirit and for your immeasurable contribution in helping me to dramatically and meaningfully rebuild my life. To my brother, thanks goes for being my very first dance partner when I was six and you were three, plus all the years you have remained my best friend even though I was not always easy to be around. Because of the support I received from the three of you not only does this book exist, but my own authentic self has been birthed into the world as well.

When you're going through draft after draft, reaching for the right words and eliminating unnecessary ones, you need friends willing to read—again and again—your efforts and offer honest and solid feedback from their personal experience of the story. This was not an easy book to read. Thanks to Deb Vaughan for being my first reader when the material was way too long and unwieldy.

To my editor, Linda Carbone, I can't thank you enough for helping me take an enormous amount of material and sculpt it down to its most perfectly rendered shape. In finally finding words I often found too many; your expert eye was infallible in cutting the extraneous so that the story became unencumbered by my need to tell it. Thanks must also be mentioned to two men who didn't know me at all but believed in my book: my publicist Scott Manning and art director Charles Rue Woods. The final product benefitted enormously from your creativity, kindness, insights and incredible generosity.

Finally, thanks to John for having the patience to wait for me to become the dance partner your skills deserve. In partnership with you on the dance floor I become my most amazing self. Thanks also for accepting me in the distorted state I was in and tranquilly waiting for me to find myself. Your love, peace and undemanding presence were instrumental in my tapping into joy and building a life around it.

These acknowledgements would not be complete if I didn't include the entire survivor community who has joined me in helping to raise awareness for Post-Traumatic Stress Disorder. The work we do together helps me achieve that long ago quest from 1981: my desire to help others not suffer the way I did. Your contributions to my own education and the development of www.healmyptsd.com have been invaluable. I thank you all—and those of you whom

I am yet to meet—for your courage, strength and powerful conviction that we do not have to live forever in the shadow of the past. I wholeheartedly agree!

Final Thoughts

Perhaps reading this book has clued you into what might be the source of your struggle or the struggle of someone you know. If that's the case, please let me help you navigate your journey. You're not alone; don't imprison yourself in isolation.

For further information about Post-Traumatic Stress Disorder, please visit me on the web. When you join our enormous online PTSD community at www.healmyptsd.com you'll have a chance to:

√ Read PTSD recovery tips on the Heal My PTSD blog
√ Listen to the experiences of other survivors
√ Hear the input of professionals trained to help you
√ Learn how to make the shift from power*less* to power*ful*
√ Strategize your PTSD journey
√ Inform yourself and others about PTSD

Also, on the site, check out these FREE offers I've designed just to get you started and comfortable:

√ **Download:** *15 Things No One Tells You About PTSD (That You Really Need to Know!)*

√ **Sign up:** Daily PTSD support emails, *Healing Thought of the Day*

√ **Show up:** Listen to my weekly radio program, *Your Life After Trauma*

You have enormous potential. The goal is learning to access it. Dig deep. You can do this. I believe in you!

Secrets of a Samurai
by Michele Rosenthal

The tragic myth is this: when you least expect it
You'll be called upon to cut your heart out,
Place it somewhere way beyond your reach, without
The body whose warmth the organ learns to covet.
When this is done, a vocal chorus will suggest that you commit
An act of self-repelling heresy: believe—beyond all doubt—
One frayed tassel of God's robe descends about
Just far enough to fully stuff and wholly fit
The aperture of your soul, which bleeds.
Today, you must choose one of two extraordinary deeds:
Accept God's gracious fingers dangling
A piece of cloth He doesn't mind you mangling,
Or shove your own hand into that small cavity,
Pull up the stronger man you've always meant to be.

*

Pulling up the stronger man you've always meant to be
You strain an unexpected muscle in your back.
In bed the next day with an attack
Of nerves, you think you can foresee
How this one act will freeze a curve in your identity
That leaves you maimed, gross as an old hunchback
Who shuffles down the street, some sad elegiac
Shell of familiarity who fades at dusk into a full transparency.
Well, isn't that your smooth Ego's joke and trip?
To make you doubt the worth of your own craftsmanship
He flips the order of the ground and the sky,
With a snap of slim fingers trains your eye
On all the fissures in the cracked concrete,

Which threaten to cripple any hint of self-conceit.

*

Threatening to cripple any hint of self-conceit
You drag yourself up from the rumpled bed,
Vow to continue as you were, instead
Of body building—after all, you're no athlete
Who seeks a new, recordable feat
Of form and discipline. No, it's said—
And you heard it—man needs one solid figurehead,
So you decide: belief in God should be complete.
Except, there exists this old, distressing, dark expanse
Of time: you gave God one, then another chance
To reveal Himself, or even, just fill up a room
That gagged and choked on its own doom.
But not a single presence came, and the rasping gasps abated,
Only because you held your breath, and so were liberated.

*

Because you held your breath and so were liberated
From all dependence, you chose the latter
Deed to guide your way. Now the matter
Staring you in the mirror you half-hated
When you hung it by a string: this weighted
Fact—it's an intangible thing you're after:
The smallest voice whose silken chatter
Flutters like an object excavated
From the dusty, cobwebbed caves of time,
An artifact so old and fragile, green with grime,
Pulling it through your lost-heart's hole
Might crush to dust what you trust to your head's control.
Stare down that glass upon the wall, and think,
I am a hero; heroes never shrink.

*

I am a hero; heroes never shrink—
You leave the bathroom sink at 8 a.m. reciting
This brand-new mantra, repeatedly inviting
The rhythm of the words to get in sync
With how your body moves, provide a link
Between your mind and spine. You're writing
I am a hero . . . 100 times, inciting
The curve to straighten out; it's on the brink.
You pause the chant to think, *So easy!*
That's when slick silence slams you like a fist.
You've kissed your last *I am* good-bye,
Now you're feeling a little queasy;
Thought your heart had not been missed—
But the beat, when you reminisce, begins to magnify.

*

The beat, when you reminisce, begins to magnify.
Its taunting music begs for you to give
Some focused thought to how you'll live
In such a stupor where instincts stultify.
In absentia, your heart can't hope to gratify
Even the slightest impulse to forgive
Sad history. Reclaiming your pulse will be imperative,
But you cut it out in a place you can't demystify.
Retrace your steps toward the sound of the pump?
The sky goes black, a cat screams, you jump
And spin, try to run in the opposite direction,
But your feet root, respond to the deep inflection
Of a voice that's calling from the concave hole—
You know that sound, that pitch, that tone: it is your soul.

*

You know that sound, that pitch, that tone: it is your soul.
The moment's come to follow through
On actions begun before you knew

The exact price for such a priceless goal.
Afraid, you doubt you're strong enough to behold
The bloody mess of such self-surgery. Then, strange déjà vu:
Your fingers itch with a wish: let them pursue
That imprisoned man who howls and hungers for parole.
You do. Up from your body's darkest crease,
He leaps to a precipice of bone and works to slip
Your heart back in its space. Piece by piece,
He explains how reinstallation will benefit
Your struggle to find, from tragic myth, release
—which, he winks, happens when you least expect it.

Michele Rosenthal is a trauma survivor who struggled with Post-Traumatic Stress Disorder (PTSD) for over 25 years. Today, Michele joyfully lives 100% free of PTSD symptoms.

The host of "Your Life After Trauma" on Seaview Radio, Michele is a mental health advocate, public speaker, award-winning blogger, writer, workshop/seminar leader and Post-Trauma Coach. For more information, visit her at **www.yourlifeafertrauma.com.**

Author photograph by Jessica Lorren

Strengthen your post-trauma journey....

Claim Your FREE
Life After Trauma Tools at
www.yourlifeaftertrauma.com/bookgifts

From nasty divorces to life-threatening experiences, stress leaves its mark. Whether you've had trauma or Trauma life's challenges can make you slow down, think and even stand still as you reassess who you are and how to move forward. To help you focus and strategize reclaiming yourself and your life, I've created the following gifts for you:

Free Ebook: *PTSD Mini-Survivors Guide*

This downloadable ebook has over 40 pages of PTSD information and education designed to immediately give you a clinical overview of PTSD itself, plus ideas for how to organize your recovery strategy. *It also contains an overview of treatment options designed to release you from the stress of any kind of trauma, large or small.*

Free Ebook: *Reclaiming Your Life After Trauma*

This downloadable ebook has 25 pages of exercises designed to help you focus on moving beyond your most challenging experience. Geared to help you see where you are, what you want and what's holding you back, it will also help you develop the right attitude for making change.

Free Audio Recording: *How To Create A Healing Intention*

Listen to this hour-long teleseminar for a step-by-step guide to creating your very own, fully personalized blueprint for going from where you are in the present to where you wish to be in the future.

Free *Your Life After Trauma Ezine*

Once a month I will send you an inspiring and practical ezine that includes tips for moving forward, plus other resources to support you along your quest to build a life of meaning, purpose and joy.

For these free gifts, visit:
www.yourlifeaftertrauma.com/bookgifts

To access free gifts, users must register by providing their email address.
Offer subject to availability.

15927341R00139

Made in the USA
Middletown, DE
28 November 2014